# RISING
# FROM THE
# ASHES

# RISING FROM THE ASHES

*Rethinking Church*

BECKY GARRISON

**SEABURY BOOKS**
an imprint of
**Church Publishing Incorporated, New York**

Portions of the interviews with Diana Butler Bass, Shane Claiborne, Brian McLaren, Peter Rollins, Phyllis Tickle, and N.T. Wright also appeared in *The Wittenburg Door* (www.wittenburgdoor.com) and are used with permission.

Cover design by Corey Kent

**Library of Congress Cataloging-in-Publication Data**

Garrison, Becky, 1961–
    Rising from the ashes : rethinking church / by Becky Garrison.
        p.      cm.
    Includes bibliographical references.
    ISBN 978-1-59627-062-6 (pbk.)
    1. Church renewal.   2. Emerging church movement.   3. Church history–21st century.   I. Title.

BV600.G37    2007
262.001'7–dc22

2007029509

*Printed in the United States of America*

07 08 09 10 11 12     10 9 8 7 6 5 4 3 2 1

This book is dedicated to anyone who has heart for the Gospel and a yearning to reach those for whom *church* is not in their vocabulary.

*"For the Christian, there is no distinction between the sacred and secular. Everything a Christian does is an expression of his faith. He does not make choices based on the religious significance of the alternative. As a Christian he makes the choice that is a logical extension of the values he has derived from his faith."*

—Mike Yaconelli[1]

1. As quoted from http://www.youthspecialties.com/yaconelli/words/wordsfrommike.php.

# CONTENTS

# INTRODUCTION

Throughout history as the culture adapted, the means of communicating the gospel shifted as well. Oral storytellers used parables and legends, as artists depicted gospel scenes through such poetic expressions as sculpture, paintings, and music. The invention of the printing press coupled with the translation of the Bible into the vernacular enabled the layperson to read the gospel teachings themselves.

In recent history, the rise of the church growth movement, which offered a seeker-friendly form of church communication, appears to be groaning under the weight of modernity. Some megachurches continue to draw crowds, though in this era of postmodernity, there appears to be a shift toward a cacophony of voices offering diverse ways of establishing community in a world that's becoming increasingly globalized. While this may appear to American eyes to be a new revolution, worship leaders in the UK have been experimenting with new expressions of faith since the 1980s.

For those looking to enter into this conversation, the plethora of books, blogs, and "buzz" words can be intimidating to the outsider. Hence, this book serves as a salon where voices come to the table. I chose people that I encountered in my years working as a religious journalist. While this list is by no means comprehensive (my advance apologies to anyone who feels slighted they were not included), this book serves as a starting point to begin to make connections.

Not all of these voices are in agreement, but this book isn't about my personal tastes. Rather, I am seeking to start a discussion about the diverse ways Christians define what it means to "be the church" in the twenty-first century. These worship leaders range from high church Celtic Christians to evangelical Anglicans, as well as a few spiritual souls who consider themselves to be postchurch. While most of the people I interviewed work on some level within the mainline tradition, I included a few US-based evangelical emergent voices who are speaking at events targeted to mainline church audiences.

This book is not intended as a cookbook where one goes looking for tricks of the trade but rather as an appetizer to whet your palate. Hence, I hope you leave the book hungry and wanting to have dinner with some of the people in the book. Once the introductions have been made, my hope is that you will continue the conversation—read the books, skim the blogs, pick up the CDs, and maybe even meet the people who are speaking your language.

Think of this book like an AA meeting. Take what works and leave the rest.

Godspeed.

# WHO'S WHO

**H**ere's the list of people I interviewed for the book, along with their self-descriptions.

**Jonny Baker** helps reimagine worship, faith, and community in postmodern/emerging cultures as part of the Mission Leadership Team of the Church Mission Society. He is a member of the alternative worship community Grace in London, coordinates worship for Greenbelt arts festival, is an author, and runs the record label Proost.

**Diana Butler Bass** is an expert in American religion who works as an author, speaker, and independent scholar.

The Rev. **Kevin Bean** is the Vicar of St. Bartholomew's Church in New York City.

The Rev. **Paige Blair** is Rector of St. George's Church in York Harbor, Maine.

**Nadia Bolz-Weber** is a lousy Christian and Theology Pub hostess in Denver, Colorado. She is planning a sacramental spiritual community for the reverently unorthodox and the irreverently orthodox in Denver starting January 2008. She blogs at sarcasticlutheran.typepad.com.

**Kester Brewin** is an author, teacher, father, and Londoner.

**Elise Brown** is Pastor of Advent Lutheran Church in New York City.

**Spencer Burke** is creator of The Ooze (www.theooze.com).

**Shane Claiborne,** ordinary radical . . . goofball . . . founder of The Simple Way.

**Tim Conder** is the Founding Pastor of Emmaus Way, Durham, North Carolina, and on the Board of Directors at Mars Hill Graduate School, Seattle, Washington, as well as the author of *The Church in Transition: The Journey of Existing Churches into the Emerging Culture* (Zondervan).

The Rev. Dr. **Steven Croft** is Archbishops' Missioner and Team Leader of Fresh Expressions.

**Isaac Everett** is a New York City–based musician, activist, and liturgical iconoclast.

**Rick Fabian** is Founding Rector of St. Gregory of Nyssa Episcopal Church in San Francisco, California.

The Rev. **Elizabeth Garnsey** is an Associate at St. Bartholomew's Church in New York City.

The Rev. Canon **Kevin Goodrich**, OP, is an Anglican Dominican priest, writer, and teacher on Christian spirituality, and serves as Canon Missioner in the Episcopal Diocese of North Dakota. His latest book is *Plugging into God's Story: A Practical Introduction to Reading and Understanding the Bible* (Xulon Press).

**Nancy Hanna** is Associate Rector at Calvary/St. George's Episcopal Church in New York City and is an advisor to Alpha USA for the New York region.

**Marilyn Haskel** is the Music Associate at Trinity Church/St. Paul's Chapel in New York City.

**Patricia Hendricks** is the author of *Hungry Souls, Holy Companions: Mentoring a New Generation of Christians* (Church Publishing) and the Executive Director of the Christos Center.

**Tony Jones** is National Coordinator of Emergent Village and the author of *The Sacred Way* (Zondervan).

**Cheryl Lawrie** works in an alternative worship project in the Uniting Church in Australia.

**Matt** is a thirty-year-old actor and a lifelong Lutheran.

**Brian McLaren** is an author and former pastor.

**Ian Mobsby** is Priest Missioner with the Moot Community, Diocese of London.

**Kurt Neilson** is an Episcopal priest and Rector of Saints Peter and Paul of Portland, Oregon.

**Jahneen Otis** is a singer, actress, and pianist whose roots are founded in the pure sounds of gospel, rhythm and blues, and jazz. She is the music director for St. Mark's Church-in-the-Bowery and the coordinator of Safari East Cultural Productions in New York City.

**Martha Grace Reese** is an ordained Christian Church (Disciples of Christ) pastor who serves as president of GraceNet, Inc.

**Peter Rollins** is a founding member of Ikon.

The Rt. Rev. **Catherine Roskam** is Bishop Suffragan of the Episcopal Diocese of New York.

The Rev. **Stephanie Spellers** is the Cox Fellow and Minister for Radical Welcome at the Cathedral Church of St. Paul, Boston, Massachusetts.

**Phyllis Tickle** is a religion analyst, writer, and lecturer.

**Karen Ward** is the Abbess of Church of the Apostles, Seattle, Washington (www.apostleschurch.com).

**N. T. Wright** is the Bishop of Durham in the Church of England and a bestselling author.

# CHAPTER 1

# Where Are We Now?

**PHYLLIS TICKLE (in person)**

**When you take the spiritual temperature of the United States, what kind of readings are you getting?**

> *Phyllis Tickle:* I don't think you can do that. I'm a great admirer of the Barna Group. There's great integrity and candor in their work. They're starting to make comments like "I'm not sure you can quantify some of this," or "You can't really tell the number of house churches." I think also that there's in Middle America a sort of moving toward the covert in mainstream Christianity. Alan Jones, Dean of Grace Cathedral, talks about how genuine or authentic Christianity may be having to hunker down under the landscape and hide until things start to cool off and then burst out like Solidarity did in Poland. I find many, many devout and previously vocal leaders in their fifties who are just not inclined to go forth and talk about their faith, though they witness quietly. They don't want to become fodder for a candidate's spiel.

**How do you define terms like "unchurched" and "believer"?**

> *Phyllis Tickle:* I have a few kids of my own who are "unchurched." That is, church per se is not where they are or where they exercise their faith. I also have some friends who tell me that church is the last place where they find God. When you use the term "believer," you must also ask, "Well, a believer in what?" At best, believer is a tired and old word. I wish we had another, better one we could use.

**How do you respond to the conventional wisdom that the mainline churches are dying?**

*Phyllis Tickle:* They are and they aren't. As Bishop Mark Dwyer has noted, about every five hundred years, the church feels compelled to have a giant rummage sale. During the last Reformation five hundred years ago, Protestantism took over hegemony. But Roman Catholicism did not die. It just had to drop back and reconfigure. Each time a rummage sale has happened, whatever was in place simply gets cracked into smaller pieces, and then it picks itself up and reconfigures. I think Diana Butler Bass is absolutely right-on when she says that progressive Christianity is that part of the established institutions presently in place that's going to remain in the center or circle around the emerging church.

In the mainline, Protestantism is losing some of its denominational lines. The Anglicans and the Lutherans are clearly in concord, for they are already swapping pulpits and acknowledging the authenticity of each other's ordination process. In all probability, the Methodists will soon be engaged in some of this. While we're post denominational, we're not post-Protestant.

When I'm talking to Episcopal audiences, I like to say, "If we're in the business of trying to save the Episcopal Church in the United States, shame on us. Judgment Day, we should be found wanting." We're in the business of serving the kingdom of God.

Funding, housing, and enabling an emergent church can lead people into a spiritual relationship and eventually to conversion. Some Anglican and Lutheran, and especially Presbyterian, congregations are quietly funding emergent forms of themselves as church plants. Presbyterians have been the most informed, wisest, and most generous in their support of the smaller congregations that are inclined toward emergent sensibilities. They see to it that such gatherings have the support they need to get started. Then, once they're off and running, the sponsoring congregation lets them loose and then goes on to support another church plant.

**What's your take on this recent "emerging church" dialogue that's happening in the United States?**

*Phyllis Tickle:* Clearly there's a new sensibility. Nobody made emergent. In fact, if you listen to Brian McLaren, about the last thing he wants to be credited with is inventing emergent. He didn't. This is not crypto evangelicalism we are looking at, but the sensibilities that have formed it clearly, I think, can be dated back to the Committee on Biblical Fundamentalism and the years from 1910 to 1915, or even farther back to the last decades of the nineteenth century when those first "fundamentalists" were meeting in Niagara Falls. There was strong recognition on their part that something was afoot that they were going to oppose with all the energy and force they could muster. At about the same time, we get that importation of what the Pew Foundation is now calling the renewalists—the Pentecostals and charismatics—whose spiritual and religious authority was experiential. As a result of these and several other factors, we had an aggressive evangelicalism in the midcentury and then, over the last thirty years, its politicalization.

Evangelicalism has lost much of its credibility and much of its spiritual energy of late, in much the same way that mainline Protestantism has. There's going to be—is, in fact—a whole upheaval, and then the landscape is going to settle back down again as it always does. We have to remember that it's not as if Protestantism came forth in one perfect or cohesive package out of Luther. Almost from the beginning, it had variants like the Confessing and Reformed movements that followed along quickly.

There is no question that part of this emergent swirl consists of those evangelicals who are looking for liturgy and a connectedness to church history, but who are not finding those things in their denominational churches of origin. A lot of the honest-to-God emerging churches are using the BCP. They are also more open perhaps to charismatic experiences than some of their forbearers were, and they are deeply involved in incarnational theology. None of those things has typically been the evangelical pattern. I'm very conscious, as well, of groups like Shared Table and Common Purse, who are returning to fixed-hour prayer, because I see the sales figures and receive the letters generated by *The Divine Hours*, which is only one among many manuals currently available for observing the hours.

## Where does doctrine fit into the growth of emergent church?

*Phyllis Tickle:* I break into an intellectual and spiritual rash over doctrine. Once, I was asked in a public forum about what I saw as the biggest impediment to spreading the gospel and, without stopping to think, I blurted out, "Doctrine." Of course I don't mean we should throw out all doctrine, but we also have to recognize its divisive qualities. Jesus did not say, "Thou shalt not believe thus so and thou shalt believe these particulars." Never! We need to find a common code of conceptualization, or we're in trouble. McLaren's *A Generous Orthodoxy* is an attempt to lay out something like that.

But it is the nature of religion to institutionalize itself, and we're not going to stop that process this time any more than we ever have in the past. There are three levels of church. There is the church universal and the church intimate. And in between them is the church institutional. And it's the business of the church institutional to connect the intimate and the universal. So we can't have an emergent movement that doesn't become at some point the emergent church institutional.

**What are some of the red flags you would like to raise as emerging church finds its footing in the United States?**

*Phyllis Tickle:* One of the things emergent has to do, and do soon, is provide some kind of seminary education, instead of simply having people lay hands on someone and say, "You're now a pastor," or having someone set up a blog with a green leaf logo and decide to regard themselves a pastor.

Another question has to do with accountability. Some of the gatherings have pastors who may or may not be a tentmaker, that is, who may be making their living elsewhere. If people only have accountability within their own group of thirty or so folk, there's the potential for going off into idiosyncratic theology and/or into a cult of personality.

Also, there obviously are all kinds of practical concerns. Where are the health benefits, for example, that allow younger men and women with small children to accept vocation? Where are the retirement programs, which is a particularly pertinent question as emergents themselves begin to mature and age?

☎ DIANA BUTLER BASS (phone interview)

**Talk about the liberal/conservative divide that you see existing in American Christianity.**

*Diana Butler Bass:* There is a real temptation on either side of that kind of binary worldview to think that the other people aren't really Christian. So, fundamentalists/evangelicals just completely dismiss the idea of there being anything such as a liberal Christian. On the other side, I think that liberal Protestants in America have (also) been guilty of characterizing evangelical Protestants. They are less likely to say that they aren't Christian, but what they will typically say is that they are not very smart Christians, that there is a kind of intellectual dishonesty with fundamentalist evangelicals, and that if only they read the Bible the right way, then they would obviously agree with liberal Christians. You can be a really serious Christian and break through all kinds of boundaries and not have to really fit with any particular label. I think a lot of people find that really refreshing. That's where I've actually gotten the most response.

**What can turn a dying mainline church into a vital congregation?**

*Diana Butler Bass:* I think it has something to do with crisis. Ninety percent of the congregations I studied were–ten or twenty years ago–on the verge of closing. They had declined so badly that there were few people left. Some of them had financial crises or crises of leadership. The vestry notes from Trinity in Santa Barbara stated that they were so divided that there had been fistfights in their board meetings! Elsewhere–sadly–a lot of clergy had misconduct cases, and (in) one of them, even lightening struck the building and burned it to the ground. So there were all kinds of crises. But I think what that means is that that's kind of the same situation in our own spiritual life. There are no atheists in foxholes and for the mainline–basically–the entire tradition has been living in a foxhole for thirty years. Some of them have realized, "Hey look, we've got to get serious here or we're going to die in this hole." Once that sense of the urgency regarding the need to change really hits in a congregation's heart, then I think that's the pathway they've opened for the Holy Spirit to be able to move in and really make a change.

**Elaborate on the relationship between the clergy and the laity in these churches.**

*Diana Butler Bass:* There is a much greater sense of shared ministry, and participation in ministry, than was ever present in the mainline churches of my youth–where we sort of still had a "father knows best" kind of church. We were the people in the pews and that was the pastor. Now, that's very much broken down, and many of these congregations have developed new patterns of what they call either "shared ministry" or "mutual ministry," or they actually resist the term "lay ministry," which is interesting. They want to call it something else because they see "lay" meaning "a nonexpert."

**Have any aspects of American culture helped–or hindered–the development of the congregations in these studies?**

*Diana Butler Bass:* If you go out and survey the sociological literature, there is sort of a dominant theme that emerges–the shift away from communal and traditional authority, be they pastors, politicians, university professors, or school teachers. This is changing to locating authority for all kinds of decisions in the life of the individual. If you had a religious or moral question in the 1950s, you could ask the schoolteacher, the pastor, the rabbi, the mayor of the town, the person who was the head of the Rotary Club or your parents, and you would get from all those different roles probably a very similar answer. There was no sort of conflict between those groups. So that was a univocal culture that spoke with one voice. Now when you shift over into a culture of individual autonomy, you do not have that. You have a multivocal culture, and you have all these different sources of authority making competing claims of truth. So, what has to happen then is that the individual has to choose which one of these things that they're going to believe in and practice in their own life to find meaning and sense of the universe in order to live a life that's worthwhile.

These are part of global changes, global shifts. Nobody is responsible for it at one level, and it seems to be just sort of unstoppable. It's just the way that it is. When you get to that point, when you say, "Okay, these changes have happened," you then have to decide what your response to them is going to be. You can say that they're evil, you can ignore them, or you can say, "This is just a culture like any other culture in which God's people have lived, and our job now is to be faithful in this changing circumstance." Once a church community gets to that point, then it opens the possibility for them to do some really serious imaginative work in reworking Christian tradition and to change context—which is what Christians have been doing since before the time of Constantine. It's really exciting work at many levels because it's sort of the deepest kind of connective work to the heart of the tradition—that tradition and culture always change. The vocation of God's people: to figure out how the gospel makes sense in each one of these successive ways that we've lived in for the past two thousand years.

**It's getting harder and harder to judge what a church is like by looking at the building.**

*Diana Butler Bass:* That's really an astonishing thing. Some of our churches look pretty traditional on the outside, but as soon as you get in, and you're there for ten minutes, you realize something completely different is going on. One of the churches in my study is a congregation in New Haven, Connecticut. You couldn't get people who were more of a stereotype of the New England Yale liberals than the people in this congregation. But they've adopted this practice of testimony. The people get up and talk about how much God has changed their lives. The pastor said that she's actually sat in front sometimes and seen newcomers just look on in shock as these privileged New Englanders get up in the pulpit. They start weeping about the way Jesus has changed them, and the newcomers actually head for the doors because they're looking for some sort of really staid, traditional New England church. As soon as you're inside the door, and you start seeing these practices displayed, there is a kind of effusive spirituality and a warmth that's very different.

## God's Politics: Not Red, Not Blue . . . Purple Churches

From the God's Politics blog (http://www.dianabutlerbass.com/blog/not-red-not-blue...purple-churches.html), November 2, 2006

*Diana Butler Bass:* For the last three years, I directed a grassroots research project on vital mainline Protestant congregations that involved "on the ground"—or perhaps "in the pews"—surveys, interviews, and field observations. In the fall of 2004, immediately before the last presidential election, I was at Church of the Redeemer, an Episcopal church in Cincinnati, Ohio. There, amid Ohio's fractious political environment, one woman remarked, "We're not really red, and we're not really blue. We're sort of purple."

Her comments rang true. Some of the congregations along my way leaned toward being blue-purples, others, red-purples. None matched any media depiction of Christian politics; none was a pure form of any political party. Mainline Protestants are somewhat politically unpredictable and do not form a unified voting block. In the 2004 elections, my team estimated that slightly more than half of the study participants voted for John Kerry, while slightly less than half voted for George Bush. Purple churches.

A liberal friend recently quizzed me on the political commitments of mainline Protestants, and I told him about purple churches. He guffawed, "Well, that's where the problem lies. Purple won't get us anywhere." He wanted BLUE churches, a mainline countermovement to the Religious Right's RED congregations. Purple, in his view, appears wishy-washy.

I do not share his perspective. Purple is more than a blend of red and blue, a right-left political hybrid with no color of its own. Purple is an ancient Christian symbol. Early Christians borrowed purple, the color of Roman imperial power, and inverted its political symbolism to stand for their God and God's reign. Christian purple—the color of repentance and humility—represents the kingdom birthed in the martyred church, unified around a crucified savior, and formed by the spiritual authority of being baptized in a community of forgiveness. By choosing purple to represent this vision, they purposefully picked a political color to make the point that their politics would subvert those of the empire.

For Christians, purple is more than a blending of political extremes, a mushy middle. Purple is about power that comes through loving service, laying down one's life for others, and following Jesus' path.

No wonder mainline Protestants are politically unpredictable. Given the issues and candidates in any particular campaign, following Jesus may take different forms at different times, involving a host of policy solutions, and balancing elements of each political party in a "lesser of two evils" voting strategy. For purple people know that God's reign judges politics, that voting is an act of Christian discernment, and that theology should critique policy. No earthly political party speaks spiritual truth.

Even though I am, like my friend, a Democrat, I hope for more purple churches—not just pure blue ones. I do not want to be part of a political movement that is the mirror opposite of the Religious Right; I want my politics to follow in the way of Jesus. So, I was glad to find that the mainline congregations in my study were not a slam-dunk for any political party. That makes them a stronger witness for grace, not a weaker one. And I was equally cheered to see a recent *Newsweek* poll (Fall 2006) reporting that the "white evangelical" vote for next week's election was running 60 percent Republican, 31 percent Democrat, and 9 percent undecided. That is, of course, significantly down in the Republican column from the last election (when nearly 80 percent of "white evangelicals" voted for George Bush). Christians should not be a voting block. Christians should be disciples of Jesus.

Mainline Protestant congregations have long been purple. Maybe evangelical churches have started to turn color, too. Could be a pretty interesting autumn—at least more colorful than 2004.

## ☎ MARTHA GRACE REESE (phone)

**Who is the target audience for *Unbinding the Gospel* and the rest of the Real Life Evangelism Series? How can churches use this resource?**

*Martha Grace Reese:* The primary audience is established churches that want to help large numbers of people get enthusiastic about sharing their faith relationally, and to start doing it. When I wrote *Unbinding the Gospel*, I assumed it would primarily be helpful to mainline congregations, but it seems to be working across a much broader theological range. As I think about it, that doesn't surprise me because the congregations from which the survey was drawn ranged from extremely conservative to very liberal. *Unbinding the Gospel* is the primary book, for groups of church leaders (pastors, elders, core leadership, evangelism teams). I've just finished two more books to support it. First, an all-congregation study version called *Unbinding Your Heart: 40 Days of Prayer & Faith Sharing* and second, a book of pastor's resources (*Unbinding Your Church*). The point of the series is to help entire churches change decades of habit—to become saturated with prayer and a real desire to share their faith.

**Is that why you feel money, sex, and evangelism are the three words that must not be named in mainline churches?**

*Martha Grace Reese:* Yea! Many mainline pastors were trained and grew up in churches where people couldn't quite articulate what they believed. They've never seen inspiring evangelism up close. Peer pressure can militate against doing evangelism. Most of our seminaries haven't taught evangelism seriously for at least two generations. Evangelism was a swear word ten years ago. This is changing. I didn't know if anyone besides my mother would read *Unbinding the Gospel* when I wrote it. We're going to a third large printing after four months. That kind of hunger didn't exist a decade ago. There are all sorts of indicators of the Spirit stirring up some kind of a wave.

**What do you see as some of the major challenges facing the mainline churches when it comes to dealing with the "E" word?**

*Martha Grace Reese:* Most of us would rather go get a root canal than think about evangelism! The cartoons of bad evangelistic practices lurk in our heads. Probably 90 percent of mainline church people react viscerally—and negatively—when you mention the "E" word. I've asked them to say what they think of when I say the word "evangelism." People call out, "Tammy Faye Bakker!" "Tracts." "People pressuring you." "I don't want to argue people into beliefs." "People should be able to make up their own minds—I don't have all the answers."

Our research showed that many of our people, including our pastors, have a hard time articulating their faith clearly. I suspect that this is because most congregations' spirituality has faded. Many of us have lost a sense of how to follow the leadings of the Spirit. So we need to allow God to retrain us in more real, functional, humble spiritual leadership, then learn how to talk about that. Our lives have speeded up so dramatically—we're formed by twenty-four-hour news cycles, constant access to the Internet, and corporate structures that move very, very quickly. It's very hard for any of us to develop a spiritual life that connects with Christ in a real and profound way. When we develop that spirituality, our lives change powerfully—when that happens AND we recognize that God can transform other people's lives, too, evangelism follows.

**How do you respond to the conventional wisdom that the mainline churches are dying?**

*Martha Grace Reese:* Many mainline churches **are** dying. The statistics in the seven denominations I studied show dramatic shrinkage. There's a continued general cycle of decline. But there are powerful spots of hope. *Unbinding the Gospel* is a call to the churches that want to turn, change, start sharing their faith and reaching new people. Thousands of those churches, large and small, are stirring out there across the country. Churches with mainline and liberal theology are making statistical turns for the better. Many congregations and denominational ministers are starting to focus on evangelism with not only integrity, but also results. After a decade of intense effort, the Reformed Church in America is on the verge of beginning to **grow** as a denomination. That's a big deal in this cultural context!

**What factors need to be present for a church to turn around?**

*Martha Grace Reese:* The absolute sine qua non is pastoral leadership. The factors I look for are: Is there a pastor with a deep spirituality who is smart enough and administratively capable enough to lead? Also, is that pastor able to stay for a long time—ten years minimum—to help do a turnaround? Is vivid lay leadership in ministry in the church? Is there the sense that the Spirit is palpable?

**How can the institutional church assist in building up pastors?**

*Martha Grace Reese:* The most important thing we can think about is how to nurture clergy leadership. It's most difficult to lead as churches have gotten smaller, demographically older, and more unhealthy. It's hard to be a pastor. They need networks of relationships and support outside of the individual church. Pastors need institutional encouragement to learn prayer disciplines, leadership skills, new models of church. Denominations can do extraordinary things to encourage pastors to experiment.

Denominations can support existing leaders. They can also do a critically important step: put major time and resources into working with very young clergy to help train them in spirituality and evangelism.

The most critical thing churches can do is to make a sustained effort at youth leadership development. Nothing that churches can do is more important than to make a fifty- to sixty-year commitment to work with high school and college age kids and train them in spiritual leadership, so they can become societal and spiritual leaders. The most painful thing I see in many of our churches and denominations is that as decline goes on, we start acting on our inherent tendency to manage what's already there. Many denominations are slowing down and stopping the focus toward kids. That's death. Give kids an experience of powerful spirituality and serving others (look at all of Mark Yaconelli's work with youth spirituality). We need to pour investment into the church's future. Take care of the youth and they'll invent the structures for the next generations.

**Words like "evangelism" and "emergent" are being thrown around like buzzwords these days.**

*Martha Grace Reese:* Those words don't fly around the mainline all that much. A lot of traditional churches are just beginning to get over great difficulties with the very idea of evangelism. That's where my work is aimed. For churches that haven't even adapted well to boomers, terms like "emergent" have barely hit the radar screen. There are reality issues. The key to evangelism is, first, to pray, and second, to follow the Spirit's leads. A specific church may not be able to reach twenty-year-olds, but they can reach forty-year olds, who can reach thirty-year-olds, who can reach twenty-year-olds. If the seventy-year-olds' hearts are turned to Christ, this can happen in powerful, miraculous ways. Each church needs to reach who THEY are called to serve and train into the faith.

If all of us were to reach the people God has put in our lives, then the dance moves in God's pattern. You don't want a sixty-five-year-old bishop pretending he's twenty-five and cool. That's never pretty! Let God lead the sixty-five-year-old, the 165-year-old churches, in the ways they can dance. It may not be an emergent. Won't be hip-hop or metal. God may need elderly First Church to swoop into a waltz.

**How do you see mainline churches working with the emerging church?**

*Martha Grace Reese:* They could come up alongside a gifted young pastor and say okay, I will mentor you. How can I pray for you? What can we do to support you? We're here and we're not going to abandon you. The biggest thing for traditional churches is to begin to care about the people we need to be reaching. We in the mainline churches need to let our hearts melt for people who need a conscious relationship with Christ. If we get to a point where we get to a deep enough level with the love of Christ, then we'll reach out to more experimental congregations with love, building space, money, prayer, mentoring, and encouragement.

**Where did you see signs of hope and growth within the mainline churches?**

*Martha Grace Reese:* I'm much more encouraged now than when I started four years of evangelism research in 2002. I'm now hearing all sorts of people saying, "Faith matters. I'm going to do something and I'm willing to change. We need spiritual practices to undergird that." "How do I share my faith?" "What do we need to do to change our habits?" I believe there is tremendous hope in thousands of congregations. It's unimaginable what God can do with that kind of willingness.

**How are prayer and evangelism intertwined?**

*Martha Grace Reese:* I don't see evangelism happening in mainline churches without prayer. I'm pretty mystically built, personally. I literally never attended a Christmas Eve service or an Easter service until I had a conversion experience in Spain when I was twenty. My own faith experience is steeped in prayer, almost certainly because I'm a true convert. I've worked with pastors and denominational ministers to develop sustained prayer lives and an openness to evangelism for the last ten years. Ministries that matters to Christ, that are ultimately effective, that are more substantial than cappuccino foam, arise out of prayer. The biggest gap in the mainline churches is that we haven't trained pastors and lay people in spiritual discipline and the understanding of the powerful, loving, enveloping presence of God.

**How do you recommend churches use the Real Life Evangelism books?**

*Martha Grace Reese:* The biggest thing I have learned about us (as pastors) is that we have this unconscious assumption that if we get some cool idea, mention it in a paragraph in a sermon, that our people will start doing it! I'm pretty clear that doesn't work so well.

The book series is in response to that assumption. We need to change habits, not just minds. We're seeing the greatest results when churches use the books in two phases. First, pastors and key leaders (elders, core leaders, evangelism teams) study *Unbinding the Gospel* in a group over an eight- or nine-week period and do the exercises. Remember, we need to change habits. That takes time and patience.

Then everyone in the congregation studies *Unbinding Your Heart* (which includes forty days of individual prayer exercises) in small groups. The people who studied *Unbinding the Gospel* either lead groups or pray in an intercessory prayer group as the whole church goes through the six-week study. We've even prepared a book to help pastors lead the congregation through the whole process: *Unbinding Your Church*. It includes sample sermons, worship suggestions, prayers, step-by-step planning tools, newsletter articles, etc., so that pastors can put their time where it matters—prayer and working with the people they're serving. It's fun—someone described the series as a "Plug & Play introduction to depth spirituality and faith-sharing"!

**What do you say to those who are looking for a quick church fix via books, conferences, and the like?**

*Martha Grace Reese:* There is no prescription—there is no one model that works. The only thing you can say that really works is to sit down with your most alive people and start praying. Start reading. Start asking questions and thinking. God will give you the next steps to take. I believe that to the depths of my soul. If we're willing to be intellectually curious and surrender in prayer, God will put the right person in our path, the right CD, the right resources, and nudge us into relationships and courses of action that will matter to God.

Anything you hear people talking about works somewhere. What I see that feels least helpful to me, particularly in the mainline context, is "here—do these seven steps and you'll be fine." That's too simplistic. I am stunned by the differences around the country of what church looks like and what works well. One of the biggest, fastest growing churches in the country is a church in Kansas City. Church of the Resurrection serves about twenty thousand people after sixteen years. They have a traditional Methodist service with a pastor in a robe. No one would say to do that. But it's working because the congregation is context-related and Spirit-dependent.

**What concerns do you see with the emerging church?**

*Martha Grace Reese:* Any time there's some rapidly growing ministry, there are all sort of contentions, struggles, distractions, confusions, crashes, and burnouts. We all need accountability. We need relationships with dear friends with whom we can be honest. Some emergent pastors are in really high-octane ministries. Some have had little formal ministry training (which has its pluses and minuses). It's easy to lose perspective. Our tendency as human beings is to split reality, especially when we're under pressure. I get some hot idea and then I want to split off from these old idiots who don't get it. We need to keep some connections with other people so we can avoid having a "Ground control to Major Tom," floating off into space (David Bowie) moment. One of the worst things that would happen to traditional mainline churches is to let emergent churches drift off to their own little planets. And the worst thing for the emergent church is to float off onto their own little planets. We need each other.

**Given that emerging pastors don't fit any typical pastor mold, how can churches help in the discernment process for those who feel called to the ministry?**

*Martha Grace Reese:* I'm going to sound very Calvinist here, despite being a Disciple. John Calvin said that there are two parts to a call to ministry: an inner, experiential call from God, and a ratification of that call by the church. I don't know how you improve upon that.

I love the fact that emergent pastors are feeling powerful calls to serve Christ, to serve people. The established church can help them (not control them, not stop them) by lovingly coming alongside the emergent pastors and helping them discern their call, and helping them in their new ministries.

If emergent pastors can find some great church that will partner with them, the church will look at the fruits of the pastor's life and ministry. Is there a growth in love, wisdom, and accountability? Is the emergent pastor reaching out to help people grow in their relationships with Christ and other people? Is s/he responsible and accountable to others? Is s/he studying? Continuing to learn everything they can about the faith? If yes, then you have an indicator that this pastor's call is real and has a shot at mattering for the kingdom of God.

Some of the emergent people are quite young and that's great. You get all this energy and power and creativity totally appropriate for them and for the age of the people to whom they're ministering. If the older people and churches can help back up the younger ones, that energizes everybody and protects everybody. For example, it helps that Trinity Church, Wall Street gave a grant to the Church of the Apostles (COTA) and certainly helps that emerging church to have that kind of sponsorship and support.

Some of the most helpful ways I've seen established people with grant money and established institutions help is to really discern with them, over time (change habits, not just minds). They're essentially mentors, saying, "I love the passion of what you're doing. Keep going. We'll help. Here are some things you might want to look at as well."

## NADIA BOLZ-WEBER (blog)

From her blog, The Sarcastic Lutheran (http://www.sarcasticlutheran.typepad .com): "Young adults . . . the elusive demographic: just light the candles and they will come"[2]

*Nadia Bolz-Weber:* The church is not unlike film and television. We all are looking for that 18–35 demographic aren't we? I was at the Rocky Mountain Synod Assembly (big Lutheran business meeting of like 540 pastors and lay leaders) over the past few days and had the chance to hostess a lunchtime conversation about the emerging church (at breakfast I told Mr. SL that I really was hoping at least 8

2. Posted on http://www.sarcasticlutheran.typepad.com, May 19, 2007.

people would show up because with less than that, it would just be awkward). There were 45 folks who showed up!—many of whom had to sit on the floor. I was amazed at the interest so I started out by asking folks to say who they were and why they chose this out of 20 so other options for lunch conversations. Many were just curious about Emerging Church, some were there because the tall tattooed lady was leading it and they were frankly curious about me, and many indicated that their churches were looking at starting an alternative worship service or a second campus geared toward the "younger generation." Here are my 2 reactions to this last group: 1) I am amazed and pleased at how much these "traditional" church folks want to reach those who are not already coming to their churches and that's a good sign that they are not entirely self-centered, which is great. 2) I unfortunately have yet to really see this work, especially if these churches are trying to reach post-moderns. If you are reading this and you know of exceptions to this statement, please let me know, especially if these churches have managed to bring in post-moderns who are de-churched or un-churched. I tried to lovingly tell of what I had seen across the country without being too defeatist about the whole thing. One red flag that goes up for me when a church wants to try and attract young adults is that there is the implication that traditional congregations are normative Christian communities which everyone SHOULD want to be a part of. I tend to resent the idea that the current manifestation of traditional church (building, pews all in a row, nicy-nice people, hymns, organ, Sunday worship, aurality as the primary sensory experience of the liturgy, etc.) is NOT a single cultural expression of Christian community but the normative expression to which all deviations are judged. My friend Annie spoke up during the conversation and said that people need to try and not see the emerging church as a resource which can be duplicated in your congregations resulting in young adults joining your church, instead folks should see these new communities as the growth of the church in a bigger sense, not simply a way to try and grow your own congregation. To this she added that established churches should support the people who are native to the postmodern culture and then walk away. Pray for the people who are appropriate to and equipped for this culturally specific ministry, see that this is a needed and vital ministry that you are likely NOT equipped or appropriate for but which is in need of resources . . . give them money, prayer and blessing . . . tell the kids who grew up in your churches, but who no longer are in Christian community to check it out. This is so needed. Now, is that it? No. What traditional churches can take from the emerging church is to pay attention to the questions that the EC is asking and then ask those same questions in your community. Please don't try and have your Easter vigil in a Goth club like Church of the Apostles. Please don't try and have a "Tomb Show" during Lent like Mercy Seat. That would be just as silly as them trying to start a "Dorothy circle" (sorry—if you're not Lutheran, that may not make sense), or start a quilting circle because it works for your community. But DO ask "is our worship service culturally appropriate to our context?" and "does the language we use in our community reflect our core values?" and "are we noticing where God is already at work in our lives and in our neighborhoods, and are we willing to join in that work?" This is what you can take form the EC: a renewed focus on mission, context and praxis. But seriously, I have no starter kit with candles, a glue on goatee and an icon for $49.95 which will attract young adults like flies on sh*t, and if anyone else claims to, please never stop smacking them.

✉ JONNY BAKER (e-mail)

**What do you think accounts for this confusion surrounding the words "alternative worship" and "emerging church"?**

*Jonny Baker:* No idea—I think it's pretty easy. Alternative worship was the name given to a movement that grew in the UK in response to developing worship that related to club culture. The earliest groups were the Nine O'Clock Service (NOS) and the Late Late Service. But via Greenbelt more groups were inspired and followed suit. Emerging church as a term came much later. I think it came for two reasons: (a) it was clear that what was being reimagined was much more than worship and (b) a lot more groups than those that had embraced alternative worship were asking questions about mission in a changing culture. Emerging church became the term used in the UK to describe that wider conversation and movement. We set up the website www.emergingchurch.info to try and collect stories of what was happening.

**Why do you define alternative worship as postcharismatic and postevangelical?**

*Jonny Baker:* That was Doug Gay that wrote that cheeky line in the introduction to our book. The term postevangelical was the title of a book in 1995 written by Dave Tomlinson. It caused quite a reaction—people loved it or hated it! Dave's point was that evangelicalism and liberalism were both responses to the modern era. Both were problematic in a postmodern culture. You've probably heard the term postliberal. Well postevangelical is making the same point. People that don't like it are committed to the evangelical word and so would want to reframe what it means to be evangelical—that's fine too. I guess it's a question of how language evolves. I personally don't use the term evangelical or postevangelical—I prefer to be Christian—that's enough for me. Postcharismatic was a provocative term as well. But I think it's honest. Many people leading alternative worship communities had come from the charismatic world. But they had moved beyond it for a number of reasons—it's culture was time warped to the seventies and eighties, it's theology was too narrow, it seemed to perpetuate an adolescent or dependent kind of spirituality with very strong/controlling leadership (ironic seeing as its early focus was on body ministry and almost the complete opposite). So post- simply means after or beyond all of that.

### context makes a difference

(http://jonnybaker.blogs.com/jonnybaker/2007/04/manifesto_follo.html, April 18, 2007)

*Jonny Baker:* one of the huge differences between the uk and us is that in the uk a lot of the emerging stuff has happened in and around the edges of the main denominations—particularly the c of e (that's the denomination i am part of so know best–apologies if i say most about that). it has a bit of a different feel than the us episcopal church for a number of reasons i think. a few of these might be . . .

1. youth ministry–the c of e invested in youth ministry in a big way and that has been the back door for renewal (a lot of the emerging people began in youth ministry and realised the problems there were actually to do with wider issues in the church).

2. charismatic renewal–whilst several new independent churches were set up in the seventies and eighties by evangelicals fed up with the denominations' rigidity, many stayed and were loyal radicals. this meant that charsimatic worship and renewal has had a big influence on worship in anglican churches albeit in polite anglican ways (led by the likes of david watson). so rather than evangelicals having to leave to get the worship and church they wanted, they simply got the right vicar and did it in the c of e churches. It's a much softer sort of evangelical on the whole.

3. permission giving bishops–for whatever reason the c of e has ended up with a number of people in leadership who see the need for new forms of church–and with the report mission shaped church and a number of other things, they have sought to encourage and create space for things to happen as part of the c of e rather than pushing them out.

4. alternative worship–this movement that grew in the uk was fairly aligned for whatever reason with denominational settings–the main exception i think was the late late service though they also did do work with the church of scotland. alt worship really was the forerunner of the emerging church conversation in the uk–people realised that it wasn't just about worship–it was also about church and mission.

5. pressure–the church numbers have been declining for twenty years. so everyone knows that the money isn't going to go round in the same way. the parish system is unsustainable particularly in rural settings where a vicar now has so many churches to oversee. all this

has created a pressure. There's nothing like pressure to fuel creativity. (the pressure just isn't on yet in the same way in the us.)

it can still be very frustrating at times but when i visit other places in the world i see how good a situation we have found ourselves in. grace, the church i am part of is a congregation of the local c of e church, st mary's, here in ealing and they are more than happy with that, as is the bishop and so on. and that's not unusual. It's a great gift.

i do think (and cms are actively encouraging) we also need stuff that is outside of those structures post church, people meeting in houses, experimental things, way out on the edge etc. renewal and change flows that way as well and in fact if it comes from both directions it is likely to be stronger. at least that's my experience.

having said that i am increasingly meeting episcopal, lutheran, pres-byterian, methodist and so on people in the us excited by mission in the emerging culture but wanting to improvise out of their denomi-national setting rather than feeling you have to rubbish the tradition in order to do the new thing. this is where emergent it seems to me from the outside is shifting and changing with openness and encour-agement to that even though it's not the roots it grew out of. i may be wrong but that's my sense of it. That's partly the reason i said it's a time for generosity and maturity because for some people who have not been part of mainline denominations they have sort of set up identity almost in opposition to mainline (that's what happened in the seventies here) so it takes some humility to realise that god is at work in those places as well when you left them because it didn't seem like he/she was. the issue of sexuality in the episcopal church or united church or whatever has heightened this identity issue in the us—some emerging people are deconstructing a lot but still think the mainline denominations are washed up on this issue (i don't want to discuss what i think about that here—it's just part of the complexity of the map). i hope i'm making sense here—i'm not feeling that articulate.

It's interesting observing the new zealand context as well. unlike the us or the uk a lot of the pioneering there has come out of baptist churches—notably led by steve taylor, mark pierson and mike riddell so the instincts about ecclesiology are different again. and in australia wrestling with denominations is played out differently again with the likes of forge having a pretty anti-institutional take, lambasting constantine for the evils of the world while at the same time people in denominations feel frustrated by that tone and get on with renewing and changing from within their set ups that they don't read as so terrible. all in all i think god is a lot more gracious than all of us and breathes life and spirit in places we have all written off a long time back. and that's a great job! in the uk i know of at least two emerging churches growing out of gay denominational settings which shows me the same thing—god is much more radical, surprising, and wonderful than most of us . . .

so blessings for the journey whatever context you find yourself in. i'm off to croatia next week to meet with some young leaders there who again have another set of challenges to deal with.

## ☎ STEVE CROFT (phone)

**What was the genesis for Fresh Expressions?**

*Steven Croft:* Fresh Expressions is the Archbishop of Canterbury's initiative for the Church of England and also the Methodist Church. The phrase "Fresh Expression of Church" was a neutral term. We wanted to find a new useful phrase to describe a collective range of phenomenon such as emerging church, alternate worship, and new ways of being church.

**How does Fresh Expressions work as a joint venture between the Methodists and Episcopalians given the two denominations are not in co-communion?**

*Steven Croft:* The Church of England and Methodist church made a covenant to work together on different areas of common life to collaborate when they can. At the local level, we're working with other denominations as well on lots of new ventures and fresh expressions of church.

We're also working at a national policy level within the two denominations with policies to support new ways of doing church are supported within the church structures. The ground has been prepared by "The Mission Shaped Church," a Church of England report that sold over twenty thousand copies, which is very high for a report like this. Also the Archbishop of Canterbury made this one of his two priorities while he's Archbishop, and he's able to provide considerable resources.

**What are the goals of Fresh Expressions?**

*Steven Croft:* We're an initiative around for five years. We want to see Fresh Expressions of church flourishing in every part of the Church of England and Methodist church and have policies to support them—for this to be normal not the exception.

**What are the principle areas of policy in Fresh Expressions?**

*Steven Croft:* We're beginning to select and train ordained pioneer ministers, who will be deployed to establish Fresh Expressions of church. Also, we're establishing lay-ministry training. In addition, we're establishing a new set of measurements to recognize parallel communities.

**Who are your other partners and how did you select them?**

*Steven Croft:* We want to work with as many people as possible. Our partners include the Church Missionary Society, the Church Army, and traditional Anglican mission agencies. We're becoming more ecumenical as we become more established.

**What have been the greatest learnings from this venture?**

*Steven Croft:* Nobody knows quite what they're doing, but there is humility of the heart, which is enabling new learning to happen. There are no experts. What is happening is that people are stepping up and responding to a call of God. A very significant number of people are being contacted in different ways through a whole variety of fresh expressions of church—most importantly through Christian service and the formation of worshipping communities. Church House Publishing put out two DVDs featuring twelve to fourteen stories so people can see the churches within the particular context.

One of the important lessons I've learned is that many of the principles that are important in beginning Fresh Expressions of church have to be applied in encouraging them. You start where you are and discern what God is already doing and then join in. So, in the US, this wouldn't emerge as the same as in a British context. Also, blessing from the senior leadership makes all the difference in launching a ministry.

**Elaborate on the resources that you have available for people interested in getting involved with Fresh Expressions.**

*Steven Croft:* We're developing our own resources because we haven't found there's anything on the shelf as it were. First, we offer a simple sequence of vision days that are running across the country where people can find out about Fresh Expressions. Next is a six-week course we run for a group of local churches where anyone with an interest in exploring missional church is welcome to attend. Then we have a one-year part-time training program in mission-shaped ministry. Teams of people, who are recommended by their local church, come together for ten evenings a year. We provide the learning materials, as well as facilitate partnerships with Anglicans, Methodists, and other denominations to get courses running throughout the country.

**What can churches do to encourage greater participation of the laity?**

*Steven Croft:* While the exercise of licensed lay ministry has been limited to supporting existing church ministries, we're looking to have licensed lay ministers deployed on behalf of the church to form new communities. I'm very encouraged by what I see. Whenever I talk to a group of lay people in this way of approaching church, they're very excited about this development.

**Aren't clergy afraid of losing their jobs?**

*Steven Croft:* As long as I take care when I'm talking to clergy to stress that the church continues to need those who are called to sustain communities, and that the traditional ministry of word and sacrament is very much needed in the development of new forms of church life, they are able to see the need to establish new forms of church for a changing culture. If I only present the need for the new, then the existing clergy can't find themselves on the map and hence, they feel very disenfranchised. I think most Church of England clergy have accepted for some time the idea of collaborative ministry. Their practice does not yet match their rhetoric, but they agree with the principle of collaborative ministry.

**What advice would you have for other denominations considering such joint partnerships?**

*Steven Croft:* It's very, very important to engage at a theological level and not just at a pragmatic level. Be prepared to engage with the interface between missiology and ecclesiology.

## ☺ IAN MOBSBY (IM chat)

(Chat with Ian Mobsby—Priest Missioner with the Moot Community, Diocese of London—via Windows Live Messenger 2:18 p.m., Wednesday, February 7, 2007)

*Becky Garrison says:* What led to the Bishop of London giving you a church for you to start Moot?

*Ian Mobsby says:* Firstly, Moot is not technically a legal church—it is a church within a church—as canon law at the moment—something called the pastoral measure only recognises parish churches—it is going to change next year

*Ian Mobsby says:* The bishop ordained me, as he recognised the importance of Moot as a fresh expression of church, and one that needed support and encouragement—and to support its ability to grow

*Ian Mobsby says:* in the context of being a fresh expression of church

*Ian Mobsby says:* Moot takes its identity from a mixture of being an alternative worship community, new monastic order (hence a rhythm of life) and desires to be a cafe church—a church mission in its own right soon

*Ian Mobsby says:* SO he ordained me—as he recognised a priestly calling—I had finished an MA in pastoral theology and ministerial education—so I was ready to be ordained.

*Becky Garrison says:* OK. How do you see fresh and emerging expressions of church being Anglican?

*Ian Mobsby says:* That's the subject of my dissertation—a huge issue I will try to summarise the head lines

*Ian Mobsby says:* 1. my research identified aspiration to be church informed by trinitarian theology—about being a church with unity in diversity—of differing traditions working together—sometimes called a mixed economy—this resonates with the writings of the Anglican divines at the time of the formation of the church of England—particularly Richard Hooker

*Ian Mobsby says:* 2. they hold a sacramental understanding—holding onto foundational views of new approaches to the ministry of word and sacrament—but go further and see that much that is done in terms of worship mission and community (function of church) desires God to be made present

*Ian Mobsby says:* 3. They practice a theology of presence—seeking to make God present in the local, national, in fact at lots of levels. Many of the fresh expressions use names that are akin to context. therefore attempting to be church and practicing the presence of God.

*Becky Garrison says:* Wow—thanks.

*Ian Mobsby says:* 4. They seek to be counter fundamentalist—that they seek to live out a place of unity in diversity and challenge the danger of fundamentalist edges.

*Becky Garrison says:* Holler when the summary is over as this is fascinating and I don't want to interrupt.

*Ian Mobsby says:* done

*Ian Mobsby says:* other thing—they seek to be ancient:future in vision

*Ian Mobsby says:* and seek to be in but not of postmodernism

*Ian Mobsby says:* sorry now done.

*Becky Garrison says:* Gotcha—What do you say to those that given the priesthood of all believers all should have equal participation at the table?

*Ian Mobsby says:* long answer coming.

*Becky Garrison says:* OK . . .

*Ian Mobsby says:* 1st need to start with models of church—my research indicated they were a mixture of mystical communion model and sacramental model . . . a fusion of the two drawn on an idea that the model of church is reflected in how the trinity models community, participation . . . the model of leadership is more of turn taking—Greek orthodox call this the perichoesis of God—literally God dancing—in dancing

*Ian Mobsby says:* people take it in turn to lead . . . so there is something important here about the body of Christ as a fluid participative community . . . so the question is what is the difference between the ordinary and ordained priesthood

*Ian Mobsby says:* So the difference then is one of function not of power and hierarchy—but one of service—that yes the bishop is the sign of the unity of the local church—they are at the bottom—and the individual priests serve the various churches—that hold up the particularly spiritual communities. With this idea—people are given room to exercise different functions of service—but all are equal

*Ian Mobsby says:* and there for all are part of the laity—the people of God.

*Becky Garrison says:* Any other thoughts on how you see ritual as being redefined for the 21st century?

*Ian Mobsby says:* well that's a lot about postmodernism—which is a move back to an image base culture rather than a word based one—driven by TV and advances in information technology—we now have a culture of mysticism created by the ever flows of information technology—a culture of spiritual tourists or searchers—where symbolic meaning has replaced words—so in that context ritual and the image and drama

*Ian Mobsby says:* find a new place—that resonates with the more mystical aspects of culture—but where we need to reframe some of the symbols and words—like King—doesn't resonate—and sounds out of date—so trinity becomes creator redeemer and sustainer for example—less male and less anachronistic . . .

*Ian Mobsby says:* we need to reframe the Eucharist—use of the apoplectic tradition for example becomes important—moving to more post Christendom models of church and post patristic forms of the governance will be the challenge of the church

*Ian Mobsby says:* so we find ourselves in a new opportunity of engaging with new forms of mysticism in our culture—which the church has resources for—and that our model of diversity and turning to understandings of the church drawing on the character of God—helps us reframe the church from institution to community, Eucharist from control to grace, from power priesthood—to powerless priesthood—the

*Ian Mobsby says:* post Christendom perspective is key . . .

*Ian Mobsby says:* end

*Ian Mobsby says:* sorry—last bit

*Ian Mobsby says:* the need to draw on the ancient—labyrinths and premodern resources—to inform the postmodern are vital.

*Becky Garrison says:* No apologies needed. Good points.

*Becky Garrison says:* How do you work within the confines of the Anglican book of prayer and the church hierarchy?

*Becky Garrison says:* esp. as you relate to your bishop.

**27**

*Ian Mobsby says:* Well—in the Church of England we now have Common Worship—which is about giving permission for experimentation—being explicit when things are set and what can be played with—so we have moved on from just the Book of Common Prayer. So we are faithful to that but do reframe it and add stuff which as permitted

*Ian Mobsby says:* regarding the bishop—we take inspiration from St Francis and St Benedict—

*Ian Mobsby says:* the models of church they built were of monastic orders—a critical way of having a radical movement—which wants to live out something new—but maintains accountability to the Bishop through a service of commitment and a relationship to it—so here you balance being radical and new with permission and accountability—new monasticism is a recreation of an old solution—you can get Moots' rhythm

*Ian Mobsby says:* of life from the Moot blog site tool bar—and you can download it from there.

*Becky Garrison says:* Why do you feel the emerging church dialogue has been going on for years in the UK, while it's just starting to catch on here in the United States?

*Ian Mobsby says:* because there is more of a crisis in the church in the UK than there is in the US—we are slightly ahead of you in the postmodern context—and this is why Australia and New Zealand are ahead of us both—as they have an increasingly post Christian postmodern culture—the key is new forms of spirituality and namely mysticism that have replaced traditional forms of Christianity

*Ian Mobsby says:* this is why the emerging church seeks to engage with new forms of mysticism expressed in culture.

*Becky Garrison says:* What would you say to US clergy who want to branch out but have a bishop that confines them?

*Ian Mobsby says:* I would say don't.

*Becky Garrison says:* LOL.

*Ian Mobsby says:* accountability is key

*Ian Mobsby says:* for me it has been about finding a language they understand—my bishop understands monasticism and the catholic language of contemplation and modern interpretations of friars—which is what we seek to be—and he gets it—you need to think about the ancient:future perspective so that they don't think you are selling out to consumerism

*Ian Mobsby says:* it's taken a while with my own bishop

*Ian Mobsby says:* but worth it—if you're serious about Anglicanism—God finds a way . . .

*Ian Mobsby says:* the bishops have an important and difficult job—they just need to find a postchristendom understanding of their role

*Ian Mobsby says:* my bishop is very wise and supports innovation—once he trusts you—and that has to be respected

*Ian Mobsby says:* Anglicans need to have a vision of looking forward not looking backwards—fresh expressions have done this for the church of england in some degree—I used to be the lunatic fringe—but fresh expressions is the vision of Rowan Williams so it has become central to the mission of the church

*Ian Mobsby says:* there is hope then.

*Becky Garrison says:* Anything you want to comment on re: your relationship with Fresh Expressions?

*Ian Mobsby says:* excellent relationship—emerging church was the front runner of fresh expressions in the cafe—yes it is a mixture of inherited and emerging churches (differing in contextual theology) but are all engaging with mission

*Ian Mobsby says:* some grumble—but I think there is good partnership.

*Becky Garrison says:* Anything you want to say about the practicalities of doing services at Moot so that the entire community is involved?

*Ian Mobsby says:* we have modeled and patterned a way of doing this—the first Tuesday of the month is a community meeting—for people to explore issues and plan services—each time—2 different people lead our non-Eucharistic service—so it is very participative—so it is lay run—and this is the way it should be—if you want to be a healthy participative community you need to build this though

*Ian Mobsby says:* participation—so that is about priests letting go of too much power—and trusting communities—but it needs patterning—check out our events to get some idea . . . we also use a wiki site for the community to self organize—bottom up rather than top down model of church—it is very possible

*Ian Mobsby says:* just means that some services are not quite what you may want—sometimes crap sometimes good—but that is what happens if it is truly communal and participative—I feel quite strongly about this . . . priests need to learn to become facilitators—like being a conductor or gallery overseer—not controller—its an important distinction.

*Becky Garrison says:* What will US worship leaders learn from attending Greenbelt UK?

*Ian Mobsby says:* how worship depends on the skills of your community—getting away from leaders who do it all—which becomes dull and monochrome—alternative worship has much to say

*Ian Mobsby says:* worship needs to be participation not some form of passive activity—so Greenbelt is a celebration of all different ways of working this out—particularly the new forms of worship programme that I have some involvement with.

## KESTER BREWIN (blog)
### A Complex Christ for an Emerging Urban World

From Kester Brewin's blog, The Complex Christ (thecomplexchrist.typepad .com), 2004:

*Kester Brewin:* Bill Clinton is perhaps not the most obvious place to start an article about emerging church (and perhaps I shouldn't have been quite so surprised to hear something quite profound coming from the mouth of a former US president) but in a recent interview on the BBC's Panorama program, Clinton said something that really caught my ear. In a series of answers to questions about his thoughts on the war in Iraq he said that he thought that unilateralism was always a mistake, and that he had always considered a key test of any of his policies was the extent to which they "aided the movement towards a more interdependent world."

Regardless of the extent to which that was actually true in practice, what made me sit up and listen was this desire for interdependence springing up in yet another place. I had just put down a copy of a flyer for a series of events at the Institute of Contemporary Arts entitled E-merge:

> "Presented as an integrated performance, the event involves presentations from the collaborating team and subsequent demonstrations of the performance system that communicates rules to different networked groups of dancers, musicians, creative technologies and audiences. These will be linked live, via purpose built innovative software and hardware technologies. Each group will influence and respond to each other's activities on stage in real time, demonstrating the powers of Emergence and generating living art organisms."

Integration, Collaboration, Network . . . It seems that the principles of interdependence, of collaboration and integration of previously discrete disciplines or power-blocks is infecting every aspect of our lives, from politics, to art, to science, to technology, sociology . . . and, as I argue in my book *The Complex Christ* (renamed *Signs of Emergence*), theology. The more I listened out for it, the more I began to

**31**

recognize the frequencies of emergence and its associated science of "complexity" resonating in more and more diverse areas.

Complexity is all about systems that are effectively self-organising. Because of their interdependent, networked structures, they don't need top-down hierarchies to evolve. Rather, through sharing information at a low level (as opposed to channelling it up and down to some "queen bee" controller) these systems are highly adaptable, flexible and dynamic. Our brains are an excellent example of such a system: there is no one "super-cell" telling all the others what to do. Ant colonies are built around the same principles. There is no "queen ant" passing instructions about what work needs doing; individual ants work this out for themselves by interacting with each other. Other examples of systems that show similarly "complex," bottom-up structures are our cities, where nobody sits around making sure enough bread will be brought into London each day, and the internet—an information system specifically designed to have no centre, and thus be indestructible in the event of nuclear holocaust.

It was initially through thoughts about organisation and leadership that steered us at Vaux to explore these concepts. As a community of artists, urban planners, policy makers, educators and writers we too began to see how the ideas spilled over and beyond traditional disciplinary lines.

In Claude Levi-Strauss' classic anthropology *The Raw and the Cooked*, he explores culture of the Brazilian Bororo tribe through their myths about food, water and the stars. He begins with one "key myth," and carefully plots and codes all the other myths from this foundation, creating a wonderful "symphony," as he puts it, out of this root melody. It is only at the end of the book that he subverts the reader by explaining that in fact it was irrelevant which myth was the "key myth," and that all the others could equally have been chosen. Regardless of one's starting point, it appears that one could explore the same ground.

This has been our experience of dealing with "complexity" and "emergence" within Vaux. We began to unearth and share our experiences of "hearing" complex frequencies resonating in our different disciplines: a shift from mainstream political party membership to grassroots campaigning, from schools as places simply to impart facts to resource centres for all learning in the community, from cities as purely economic beasts networked communities where place and locality are vital . . . And from a top-down, Temple bound God to the emergent, complex Christ.

This was the sound resonating through all of these things: the ison, the elemental frequency, the universal background radio noise of the Spirit. While scientists in the fifties claimed new "discoveries" of complexity, two thousand years previous, God had undergone a radical metamorphosis, a re-emergence that saw "Him" vanish from the high, hard entombing Temple and re-incarnate as a single sperm, with only enough energy to breech the walls of a tiny ovum. Living for a short time, even this life was extinguished. In a desperate attempt to control this divinity going critical, we put Christ to death, unaware that this very act broke the phial, smashed the glass and released the virus of the Spirit.

This is what we celebrate when we break the bread and share the wine: Christ's body, centralised, located physically in one place, is broken and distributed amongst the gathering of believers who then disperse. The elements are internalised, made invisible. The distributed body is thus taken out to infect the community. Unseen. Not controlled by a temple, not dictated by a hierarchy. The network of the Spirit is spreading like yeast through dough. It cannot be pared from the community it lives among, it cannot be singled out and destroyed, branded sacred or secular.

Christ's "complexity" forces us to radically re-assess the boundaries of what we call church. Which power structures and hierarchies are really relevant? How can we distinguish who is "in" or "out," what is "clean" or "dirty," what is "true" or "untrue." Without the dictators we so easily default to we are forced to take mature responsibility for our development as communities of believers, and consider our place in an emergent world. It is my belief that in doing so we will see this virtuous circle appearing:

> In the move from Old to New Testaments we see God re-emerging as a bottom-up, complex divinity, and the body of Christ as a distributed network of the Spirit.
> The cities we live in are complex, emergent structures.
> The city is the place where the divine and the human are most clearly seen in partnership: human hands take divine soil and build structures of stone and glass.
> Thus the city is the very place where a complex, emergent church can find its most natural habitat.

It seems to me that the alternative worship movement is perhaps the natural locus for the development of worshipping communities based on these principles. We are not there yet—indeed, it would be foolish to equate many of the "emerging church" activities we hear about with this Emergent Church that I believe we must seek.

The science is still new, and, given that places such as the ICA are still exploring, the ideas still fresh. This is not a time for train-spotting culture and following twenty years later. It is time to be the train. To begin to model creative, emergent, complex communities of faith rooted in the urban experience to the rest of the world. A world which, as Clinton recognised, is still trying to find an interdependent way forward from the ruins left by unilateralist hierarchies, in just the same way as many Christians are trying to find a conjunctive way forward from the narrowly focused fundamentalist experiences that have ultimately left them needing more. An emergent faith is not wishy-washy liberalism by another name. It is a serious attempt to move beyond hard-line positions to a place where we understand the inter-dependence and inter-relation of things. We must therefore ensure that the back-drop to our movement is not a limp screen of "trendy postmodernism" lit by a dim tea-light of reactionary flight, but a seri-ous engagement with culture and thought, resonating with the ison of the Spirit that calls the body again to re-imagination and re-configuration based on God's radical, bottom-up principles.

*My gratitude to Kester Brewin for his book and for raising so helpfully the questions which we must address if the aspiration of being a "Mission Shaped Church" is to go beyond rhetoric. Along the way of the "Complex Christ" there are some suggestive meditations on scripture informed by patterns and images drawn from the natural sciences. This is conjunctive bible study at a point in which we are finding the compartmentalising of the intellectual universe, regarded by Weber as the essence of modernity, increasingly unsatisfactory.*

—Rt. Rev. Rt. Hon. Richard Chartres, Bishop of London

## ☎ TONY JONES (phone)

**Describe Emergent Village.**

*Tony Jones:* Emergent Village is a collection of innovative church leaders who are attempting to renew the church and the Christian faith for a postmodern world.

**What kinds of people do you attract to Emergent Village?**

*Tony Jones:* The people we attract are those who not threatened by hard questions and confident in who they are, but similarly they're a bit disenfranchised in the institutional ways people are being Christian. If you're willing to roll up sleeves and see what's it's going to take to redeem or overthrow these organizational church structures, then you'll probably find a home with a lot of peers.

**Is EV for everyone?**

*Tony Jones:* If you come representing a group and you're not willing to be personally deconstructed and answer very deep questions about your motives for ministry, you'll have a hard time hanging around Emergent Village.

**What can existing churches and church plants learn from each other?**

*Tony Jones:* Church planting has to be an entrepreneurial venture. Successful church planters tend to be highly competent people, who get

**35**

things done. People who plant successful churches would never work in bureaucratic institution. I don't know if people who have defined themselves by their confessional doctrine can understand what we're doing. It takes a mainliner being willing to say yeah being Anglican is not the defining issue of my Christianity but being a lover of God is how I define myself.

### How do you deal with the criticisms that EV is mostly white straight males?

*Tony Jones:* We aim for diversity on our Board of Directors and our Coordinating Group. Emergent Village worked very hard to become more diverse. It's an uphill struggle as most pastors are white. Also, we aim to treat all people with respect and grace regardless of theological stance on issues such as homosexuality. We feel friendships trump theology.

### What are the ways that people can connect to this emergent church discussion?

*Tony Jones:* With the advent of new media, we can connect with people very easily. Everyone can have their own voice via their own blog, which is a beautiful thing. Also, podcasting is a valuable resource. Macs have cameras built in, so live web chatting will be next. A local emergent cohort can have a guest speaker via live web cam. Also, there are emergent events all the time. These face-to-face meetings cement the bonds between people. Emergent people tend to be relationally manic people. It takes some people a little extra to go into an event or a pub and elbow their way into group and start throwing down smack on spirituality or theology.

### How do you deal with the concerns that in an emerging structure anyone can set up a blog and say they're a church planter?

*Tony Jones:* People set up fake churches all the time. If you've got something to say and you're a decent writer, people will read your blog. I have a buddy, who goes under the name Postmodern Negro (http://www.postmodernegro.com). He work for the IRS and is one of the most emergent bloggers out there. When he writes, it's wicked and a lot of people tap into his blog. The cream rises to the surface. This is not an academic guild where you have to whip your package on table just to remind people you're a man like Lyndon B. Johnson. We ask how people are doing and care about their lives.

## ☎ TIM CONDER (phone)

### What's your role with Emergent Village?

*Tim Conder:* I have been involved with Emergent as a leader since its inception and also as a leader in its earlier incarnations. Over the years I've helped host theological conversations (the Hauerwas event in Durham, North Carolina) and developed the first cohort team to help our local conversation groups (or "cohorts") get started. This has truly been a labor of love. I have always been passionate about the vision and values of Emergent. There has been true friendship and community among its leaders.

### How does emerging church interface with the liberal/conservative church scene?

*Tim Conder:* Your typical emerging church leader does not fit into that liberal/conservative dialectic, but so many institutions set up this dialectic. The evangelical paradigm is that we often don't want to work with people not in doctrinal agreement, whereas the mainline paradigm was concerned about pedigree and tradition. Many emerging churches are led by people who would not fit the definition of anyone who is well trained in ministry. On the other hand, I have a guy in our congregation who has been a senior pastor in the mainline church for twenty-five years. What his congregation wanted to do was very far from what he wanted the gospel to do. So now he runs a café in town and uses it as a community springboard. The liberal/conservative divide is a great challenge for the emerging. We recognize that the two Protestant "denominations" embrace critical portions of the gospel while also ignoring other elements. Our passion for the gospel compels us to work in partnership with both tribes while honestly trying to avoid this polarity.

### How does someone connect with this movement?

*Tim Conder:* It's not been hard to get involved with the emergent movement up to a certain point. So far, the growth of emergent has been like the era of westward expansion—put a leader in the wagon train and head west! Most of our events have been conceived of and lead by a team of volunteers who were passionate about the mission of the event. Our local cohorts are developed by individuals and groups of friends who have a passion for this conversation. The emergent community has formed and grown through local groups, a few events, online, and in the wake of our writing. Certainly, Brian McLaren has played a huge role in raising the conversation that has engaged so many.

**Can you elaborate on the different streams within the emerging church?**

*Tim Conder:* I see five different streams—a Reformation stream, a post-Reformation stream, the new monastics, transitioning churches, and a postchurch stream. The Reformation stream is exploring new methodologies and new arenas of mission while maintaining an allegiance to the modern, reformed systematic. I would place myself very much in the post-Reformation stream of emerging church. Without rejecting our modern theological roots entirely, we are very sacramental—and very enthusiastic about pre-Reformation Christianity and pre-Christian Judaism. The new monastic and postchurch streams are far enough outside the realm of the church that they're influencing everybody. Transitioning churches are becoming more common—fellowships where an emergent Christianity is forming in tension and dialogue with late modern Christianity. There's a great diversity developing and a tug of war for what's the real emerging church.

**What can liberal and evangelical churches learn by partnering together?**

*Tim Conder:* The liberal/conservative cold war that's lasted one hundred years and divided Protestant Christendom is ending in postmodernity. The philosophical rationale for the differences is eroding. This presents a great opportunity for dialogue. In that very divisive cold war, both communities held on to portion of the gospel but not the whole gospel.

**How does culture interface with the emerging church?**

*Tim Conder:* Emerging church is deeply organic and very different based on its context. The church emerges out of a specific community and the boundaries of that church are shaped by that community to address those needs. So much less so than many common forms of Christianity, the emerging church is far more suspicious of the language of measurable outcomes, setting numerical goals for growth, or developing centralized organizations.

**Could you summarize the fears existing churches have regarding the emerging church's interaction with culture, and what can be done to alleviate these fears?**

*Tim Conder:* One of the points I made for people in existing churches is they've got to understand that the gospel that they teach is affected and impacted by culture. Their gospel is not culture free. This simple realization can pave the way to dialogue with emerging churches. The emerging churches can in some instances be so culturally drawn and so interested in hearing God's voice in culture that they let culture trump the historical church when it suits their purpose. I would caution emerging churches not to let the limbs of culture overwhelm their viewpoint.

### How do you define mission?

*Tim Conder:* The mission of the church has always been impacted by culture. When colonialism began to discover non-Christian lands, missions and evangelism were birthed in modern definition of Europe colonizing a premodern world. They saw mission as the work of professionals. We need to see mission as a whole life posture. Christianity is missional at its core. Most importantly, the mission is participating in God's agenda, rather than our self-derived agendas (often well-intended but also regularly imposed of God).

### Now define missional Christians.

*Tim Conder:* Missional Christians discern God's footprints and where God is going in this world. All of this is missional whole life acts. Mission is holistic. The primary contribution emerging churches have offered to the existing church world is a much more holistic viewing of the world. Leadership in this dialogue has to be interventionistic to some degree because in mission people tend to be very passionate people and like any kind of activist, they're very quick to say why what they're doing is the most important thing to do.

### How do you handle sensitive issues like gender?

*Tim Conder:* Postliberals and postevangelicals have two different conversations coming from different conjectures. It can be very offensive for postliberals when people even entertain conversations that imply that the roles of women could be limited. In the evangelical and postevangelical world, the role of women is still an ongoing conversation. In the current moment, it is quite difficult to have the different conversations in the same context. I have been very passionate about challenging the evangelical tribe to not only acknowledge an incarnate gospel and reading of text, but to apply this to gender. Reading the texts from this vantage point truly liberates women to serve in the church in any capacity.

**Why is worship the worst starting point for churches wishing to begin a transition to an emerging culture ministry?**

> *Tim Conder:* Part of the methodological bias that they have about emergent is that people still come to emerging environments and assume this is a worship style or a worship change. The worship area of the church is the war room, where the greatest conflict and biases come into play. The postmodern transition is way more than methodology. I see worship as very significant, but when in discussion about worship styles and services, the whole programmatic and preferences co-opts the whole conversation on transition. People have agenda items that are outcome driven (e.g., need more twenties, need to grow more) that become the driving assumptions of postmodern church. I encourage people to get involved with emerging conversation to be deeply theological about how we understand these things like the atonement, as well as having reciprocal relationship with how churches that do things like spiritual formation and worship. So many pastors are so pragmatically driven that any conversation on transition inevitably gets overwhelmed with decisions about worship services and styles. In so many ways, this default ignores a more holistic understanding of worship typically embraced in emerging churches.

☎ Troy Bronsink (phone)

**How would you describe emergent?**

> I have seen in the Presbyterian Church an infatuation with the Sunday morning service and, more recently, the shifts in popular styles to such services. It has been hard, in this culture of self-stylizing consumerism to differentiate "emergent" from yet one more "contemporary-er" style. I read some of the more peripheral authors who are pursuing the emergent conversation in terms of "next generation" and less in term of ecclesiology and missiology These are great folks, but as best as I know, they are a bit nearsighted in their focus on worship styles. The only way I know how to talk about emergent is to balance this with a farther-sighted hope about missional living and how we're called to participate in the inbreaking Kingdom of God. In other words, the "how" of church is continually reshaped when the Spirit reshapes our imagination of the "why" of church. Emergent is a conversation between folks about a new post-Christendom "why."

**What are cohorts and why would you encourage church leaders to get involved with their local cohort?**

A cohort operates like an artists' guild. I am better at my craft by working with others. Every smithy in a medieval blacksmith's guild or every sculptor in an Hellenistic artists guild would express his work uniquely. And yet their work would be sharpened by such a relationship with fellow artisans. The cohort gives you a chance to admire things that are generated and created and made buy fellow co-creators in the way of Jesus. As a singer/songwriter, I love to be with other artists and hear what the other women and men craft, as "readings" of our world. Songwriter guilds observe the world through one another's artwork. From the moment I met up with the folks who would become the Atlanta emergent cohort, it was people looking to "read" everything through the lens of God's coming kingdom, even to examine institutional environments with this kind of critical eye. I know plenty of females who are rechanging the dialogue too. The discussions we're having around family and co-parenting around issues such as the complications of raising kids in education systems that are failing and yet not abandoning these systems aren't typical white male patriarchal discussions. But these are some of the questions we discuss in such spaces.

**How does ordination fit into this paradigm?**

In my Presbyterian tradition, ordination is a sign and symbol, a "material" act with "ontological" claims: God calls and enables humanity to serve creation. But, in actuality, ordination acts as much as gatekeeper and reinforcement of hierarchy as it does signification of God's call. The credentialing does bring accountability with it, however. And in this way, emergent will never be able to act as a denomination. It's a challenge, ecumenically, to say that anyone should not be ordained when the Spirit of God is baptizing them for ministry now. The problem comes when emergent builds a "street cred" that falsely adds credence to a leader in the eyes of someone new to the conversation. I can see two scenarios here: One, if a person uses any platform, such as emergent, to claim a sort of leadership mantel and yet they are not practicing habits of the way of Jesus, emergent leaders need to warn others of these fakes and powergrabbers. But a second scenario is the person lacking in leadership gifts, without clarity and focus, these kind of folks will have a hard time sustaining their "home-made" gospel and those things sort of sort themselves out. I'm not so sure emergent, or any other ecumenical relationship can or should bother itself with censuring such "fakes."

**How did the church where you serve become affiliated with the emerging church?**

The Church of St. Andrews is in Sandy Springs, a northern suburb of Atlanta that incorporated as its own city three years ago. The church is about forty-five years old and dug into the Purpose Driven church model about seven years ago seeing a lot of immediate growth in numbers. They moved into a two service model: contemporary and a traditional, and engendered an either/or approach to these services by reinforcing them within church committee structures and a polarity of theological discourse. This either/or whittled the congregation down by three hundred percent. In January 2006, they got in touch with me through the presbytery saying they wanted to be an "emergent church." But, I thought, how can a Presbyterian church, or any existing church, just conclude they want to be "emergent? I guessed that they wanted a "contemporary-er" worship style. I agreed to meet with them for discussions and coaching around emerging perspectives on the missional church.

I worked with different committees meeting with them and learning things, never thinking I would serve as a pastor this far out from downtown. Then, for five weeks through Lent and into the season of Resurrection, I "supply" preached, using lectionary texts to shape the weekly worship gatherings and sermons. And then, on Easter Sunday, something hit home for me. I was struck that the same Spirit breathed by the resurrected Jesus on the disciples was being breathed on the suburbs, on these brothers and sisters, gifting them to participate in resurrection. And I wanted in with them. It took four more months for me to separate from my consultant responsibilities and satisfy the Presbyterian procedures to become their pastor. But now I've been here for five months (as of February 2007). Today we're realizing there are a lot of traditions operating here depending on your perception of Presbyterian. It is never simple to be in transition, especially when the former orientation is rooted in a shared denominational "brand" hiding dozens of unspoken competing assumptions.

Most in the emerging church conversation take the polyvalent religious landscape for granted, but this is probably the most difficult stem cell to transplant into a 45-year-old strong body of an existing church. But the polyvalence was already there anyway, just hidden, unexamined. In working from the emerging church conversation within the traditional church, I'm having to relearn teaching tools of translation. I'm learning to trade "outside" metaphors for those domesticated "Christian" images resting within the institutional church. The jury is still out as to whether or not this changes the gospel itself. I have hope that the Spirit can still breathe life into these old bones! But I'm not assuming that it will naturally happen. We're still waiting to see.

**What can existing churches and church plants learn from each other?**

In Atlanta during the 1970s, the denominational structure of the Presbyterian church took the responsibility of starting churches from the congregations and gave it to the Presbytery (a middle governing body). On one hand, this took away from congregations the capacity for rebirth through seeing new ways of doing church. Instead, churches opted to see the others as competitors and to evaluate programs and mission in terms of competition for customers/consumers. Many churches lost the ability to see something *new* as a sign of hope for something larger than themselves. On the other hand, the Presbytery was able to plant new types of Presbyterian churches outside jurisdiction and to plant immigrant fellowships. In such cases, an entrepreneurial pastor would plant in areas of suburban growth or in areas of high ethnic denisity where Presbyterians could assimilate with similar congregants. In this sense, you can say that the Presbytery-centered approach to church planting has resulted in two separate environments, mature environments (existing traditional churches) that are closed, and immature spiritual environments (church plants) who seek maturity by realizing their own "closed" identity. Every time one such church plant matures it then has the status of existing church.

But this is beginning to shift. What we are working on recently in our Presbytery is counteracting this tendency by creating environments for risk and experiment. In September of 2006 we formed an emerging church committee that works on a "third way" of church planting. We are looking to bridge relationships between social, religious, and business entrepreneurs. We are seeking a symbiosis where an existing congregation could be taken on a date with a church plant in infant stages and given the opportunity to taste and see this innovation. In this effort we are finding people who never would have imagined participating in God's dreams in such a different (non-institutional) way. And my hopes are that Presbyterians here in Atlanta would mature through such an expanding view of the kingdom of God and the church's mission in God. That part of this closed system of denominational church growth might become increasingly generous.

# CHAPTER 2

# The Gospel of the Kingdom

 PHYLLIS TICKLE (in person)

**What prompted you to write** *The Words of Jesus: A Gospel of the Sayings of Our Lord*?

*Phyllis Tickle:* Jossey-Bass, which is a division of John Wiley Publishers, came to me with the idea. Basically, they asked what if all of the canonical Gospels were merged, what would we discover about the Jesus of the Gospels? We all know that the historical Jesus is to some extent a construct of scholarship. But nobody really knows what he actually said and what he didn't say. All we can do is guess. So what does the gospel Jesus look like when we get rid of all the duplicates and triplicates, and we lay him out historically and chronologically as best we can? Well, most obviously, the first thing you have is a sayings gospel that only contains the sayings of Jesus with the exception of a little introductory phrase such as "Jesus speaking to the disciples, said." What you also get is starkness, and yet a maturing, as he begins to more and more understand what it is he's come to do.

Now, as we all know, hundreds of people before me have made parallel gospels and narrative Bibles. I stand, certainly, on the shoulders of some of their work, but merging is a different task from paralleling. The whole exercise was a great intellectual puzzle and, in some ways, fun to do as well. For one thing, I discovered that my poor Greek, which was never very athletic, is now downright arthritic.

But in this book, I'm making the case that the historical Jesus and the actual Jesus have to be blended together in some kind of recognition that the Gospel of Jesus is the one we've got. We have to come to a point of respecting the tradition of two thousand years of Christianity that have proceeded from the received Jesus.

This book needed to happen, I suspect, regardless of who actually was to take on the work of writing it. The first shot out of the barrel seldom scores, of course. It's usually the third or fourth book on a subject that hits the target. So be it. At least the conversation has begun.

Hugh Hefner did a great deal for American culture when, in mid-twentieth century, he opened up issues of sexuality and did all kinds of iconoclastic things. I think we'd be fools not to be aware of his contributions. But by the same token, we have hardly been responsible in our use of the gifts given. We took much of the release from misconceptions and errors that we were given and used it to become libertines, not understanding that a better use of Hefner's iconoclasticism, unholy as it was in places, would have been a very studied approach not only to sexuality itself but also to what had been that was wrong in the first place and had made it possible for him to thrive.

I have a great deal of respect for the work of Robert Funk and The Jesus Seminar, but they too often function as iconoclasts. What we need to ask ourselves now is what was so wrong with what we were doing that has made this kind of iconoclasticism seem so important to us, so informing, so liberating? How, now, can we use it in a productive way? We can't work with broken pieces that are simply lying about the ground. We have to pick them up and begin to construct something with them. So I think we have an obligation, and a call to vocation, if you will, to look at Jesus in the Gospels and see what we can find as a result of the very legitimate skepticism that has come into our understanding as a result of the historical Jesus studies. But we also have an obligation not to throw out the baby with the bathwater.

Yes, we bring our intellectual skills with us, but we must also bring our heart into this debate.

☎ PETER ROLLINS (phone)

**What do you mean when you say that we must seek not to speak of God but rather to be that place where God speaks?**

*Peter Rollins:* Within my own Christian faith tradition, there has been an attempt to speak of God, and by this I mean that there has been an attempt to understand the thoughts of God. However, I think that this pursuit is misguided. There is an ancient Jewish parable that illustrates this in which two rabbis are arguing over a verse in the Torah, an argument that has gone on for over twenty years. In the parable God gets so annoyed by the endless discussion that he comes down and he tells them that he will reveal what it really means. However, right at this moment, they respond by saying, "What right do you have to tell us what it means? You gave us the words, now leave us in peace to wrestle with them."

In this parable the rabbis do not want a God's eye view because, even if that were possible, that is not the point of faith. Faith seeks to transform reality rather than merely describe it. The parable works from the tradition that states that one must wrestle with the text in every context, rethinking it and learning afresh from it like a piece of art rather than treating it like a textbook to be mastered.

The desire to get a God's eye view of the world is reflected throughout history in theology, mythology, and philosophy. In much of the Western intellectual tradition there's a strong desire to name and capture God in conceptual form. I am trying to explore the ancient idea that God transcends all names. We can't reduce God to a theological idea without making an idol out of words. Instead of thinking of God as a noun, it is perhaps more useful to think of God as a verb. For God is known through action. To say we need to be the place where God speaks means that we need to be the place where God moves through the world. We have to endeavor to be that place where we embody the life of God instead of merely talking about God.

**Elaborate on this statement, "Such fissures of God as depicted in the Old and New Testaments help to prevent us from forming an idolatrous God, ensuring that none of us can legitimately understand God as God really is."**

*Peter Rollins:* What I'm trying to get at there is that God, as presented in the Bible, escapes our attempts at capturing him in conceptual form. This happens in two major ways. First, we cannot grasp God, not because there is a lack of names, but because there is such a surplus of them. These different ideas and names of God clash at various times, for instance when God is named a warrior and then a peacemaker or one who is unchanging and one who rethinks situations. The fact that there are so many ways of naming and describing God is a way of saying that no name or group of names can grasp God. Second, there are those moments within the Bible when God appears in a way that refuses any name whatsoever. Both of these strategies seem to fight against the desire that many have to place God into words as witnessed in the Kabbalah tradition where there are lots of names for God such as the Monogrammata (the one letter names of God), the Diagrammata (the two letter names of God), the Tetragrammaton (the four letter name of God), the Octagrammaton (an eight letter name of God), and the Decagrammaton (a ten letter name of God), as well as the twelve, fourteen, twenty-two, thirty-three, forty-two, and two hundred and sixteen letter names of God. All of which pale into insignificance when compared to the massive three hundred and four thousand eight hundred and five letter name.

**Some would say this sounds un-Orthodox.**

*Peter Rollins:* Well that all depends on where you stand and how you define orthodoxy. The word today has taken on a rather unhelpful Enlightenment-influenced definition as "correct belief"–the ability to affirm a certain creedal formation. However, in the more ancient tradition the doxa of orthodoxy does not refer to belief but rather to praise. We see this in the word doxology, which doesn't mean belief, but rather worship. So, orthodoxy actually means correct praise not correct belief. In that kind of a way, it becomes less about the affirmation of a theological approach–important as theology is–but a way of being like Jesus. We have to rediscover this idea that orthodoxy isn't belief oriented but praxis oriented. In this way the approach I outline isn't unorthodox if it helps to bring people back to wonder and praise . . . whether it does or not is of course open to question.

**What then is the task of orthodoxy?**

*Peter Rollins:* The answer to that is simple, and yet infinitely complex, for to be orthodox is to bring praise to God through one's life. While people these days are asking the question, "Is Christianity true?" the more fundamental question must be, "What does Christ means when he uses the word truth?" The reason I am asking that question is that when Jesus talks about the truth, he talks about life. The truth is what brings life. My axiom for today is that Christianity at its core doesn't explain life, but it brings life. We must thus ask whether our beliefs and actions bring life, healing, and love to the people in the world. To bring love into the world is to know God for God is love. This is not the knowledge of creeds and theology but the knowledge of a transforming relationship with the source of all love. Truth in Christianity is thus different from the way we understand truth in the world, for the truth of Christianity is life, not description. This is why I talk about heretical orthodoxy, i.e., someone who does not understand God yet who changes the world in love.

**What then does it mean to be a Christian?**

*Peter Rollins:* It means entering into a journey of becoming one. It does not mean accepting a worldview but rather entering into a healing journey of life. To be a Christian also means that one is committed to exploring this life through the Judeo-Christian tradition, wrestling with it, learning from it, and being transformed by it. Being a Christian means learning how to be the opening of life into the world.

**Why do you call Jesus a subversive prophet who signaled the end to all religious movements?**

*Peter Rollins:* One of the interesting things about Christianity is that Christ both founded a religion and yet signaled the end of all religions. Jesus said there will come a time when we worship in spirit and in truth rather than on one mountain or another. The parable of the mustard seed grasps this. It speaks of a seed becoming a tree that will provide a nest of birds. The traditional interpretation is that this tiny movement will become an institution that will house people. But then there is another interpretation that says that the birds of the air are symbols of evil. In this reading the movement will grow into an institution that will house that which stands opposed to God. What if neither interpretation is true but rather they both are. In Christianity, we need both the priest and the prophet. If religion loses the prophet, it can become prideful and arrogant. If it loses the priest, then you end up with nothing but silence. Christ can thus be seen as founding an irreligious religion, i.e., a religion that critiques the idea of religion, a religion without religion. This is one way of understanding deconstruction.

## BRIAN McLAREN (in person)

**What is the real scandal of Jesus' message that you explore in your latest book *The Secret Message of Jesus*?**

*Brian McLaren:* It's that he isn't talking about just going or not going to hell after you die. He's talking about a radical different way of living. He's talking about changing the world and living in a subversive and radical way in this world. That's what his pregnant phrase "kingdom of God" involves.

**As you finished *The Secret Message of Jesus*, what was the biggest learning for you about the kingdom that you didn't know beforehand?**

*Brian McLaren:* I began the book with the hypothesis that the message of the kingdom was at the center of what Jesus taught. By the time I was done I was convinced it was in the center of not only what he said but also what he did. Obviously parables are short fictional ways of describing the kingdom, but as I wrote the book I came to understand that miracles as signs of wonders of the kingdom, and I understood the crucifixion and resurrection as a prophetic dramatization of the kingdom. The pervasiveness of it really hit me. I ended the book with more questions than I began with regarding how the message of the kingdom relates to eschatology. I'm still thinking that area through.

**How did your book *Everything Must Change: Jesus, Global Crises, and a Revolution of Hope* advance your thinking of the kingdom of God?**

*Brian McLaren:* What I want to do is take the idea of the kingdom, which I tried to make as clear as I could in *The Secret Message of Jesus*, and then I want to try to apply that message to our contemporary global crises. I'm going to talk about different ways that our civilization is set up in terms of ecological suicide, religious suicide, political suicide, and economic suicide.

**Speaking of contemporary situations, let's talk about the challenges you see as the church moves from modernity to postmodernity.**

*Brian McLaren:* There is so much argument about the word postmodern that the first thing I say is that people should be careful about reducing a very complex subject to a one dimensional kind of binary opposition where you throw everything into a blue modern bin or a green postmodern bin. I've always said that life is much more complex than that. Besides, in the last couple years, I have become more convinced that a better word than postmodern is postcolonial.

**How come?**

*Brian McLaren:* As soon as you start talking about postmodernism, people want to argue about theories of knowledge and certainty, a field called epistemology. You end up with layers and layers of thinking about thinking about thinking about thinking. That's not unimportant, but it's certainly not the whole story. The other side of the coin is to talk about the ways claims about knowledge and certainty are used to fight or perpetuate injustice. And that's the postcolonial discussion: looking back on five hundred years of colonization by so-called "Christian" nations and asking, "What were we thinking? How did we justify the terrible things that were done? How can we be sure we don't do that sort of thing again in the future?"

The real issue, in my mind, is not simply an argument about truth; it's the need for repentance about the abuse of power—especially by white Christians who used the Bible to justify some pretty horrific things, whether we're talking about the genocide of native peoples, the African slave trade, the Holocaust, apartheid, or whatever. While we claim a high level of certainty in regards to matters of truth, we have shown ourselves to be relatively clueless about matters of justice. I'm not advocating uncertainty at all; I'm all for having a proper confidence, but I also want us to think about how we can be more gentle and humane in the way they treat other people, especially people whom we feel don't see the truth as we do.

## So, where does emerging church figure into all of this?

*Brian McLaren:* There's so much going on, and people are at all different places. I mean, I started asking certain questions fifteen years ago, and one question led to another and another, and here I am now. Other people are just asking the first set of questions now, or they're asking the questions in a different order. But what all of us have in common, I think, is this sense that we're trying to be faithful to God in the aftermath of modernity and colonialism and all that they entail.

## How come so many liberal clergy never talk about Jesus? It's like they're afraid to say his name.

*Brian McLaren:* I think a lot of them are reacting to fundamentalism and the Religious Right. Enough angry folks have hurled the word "Jesus" around like an insult that other folks don't want to say his name at all. It almost feels to them like a racist or a hate crime statement sometimes because "Jesus" is used to legitimize all kinds of fear and intimidation. Another reason goes back farther in history of liberalism where I think people were seeking to speak in more theistic, deistic, universal, non-particular, nonspecific ways. They had reasons for this in the 17th and 18th centuries, with all the religious wars in Europe, but I think that tide is going to change because of the work of people like

**51**

N. T. Wright and Steve Chalke, who are helping us get a new vision of what the message of Jesus is. I think if we could get that back, people are going to be very excited to talk about Jesus again.

**How does the church deal with complicated issues like homosexuality?**

*Brian McLaren:* I think a big part of our challenge is to realize what other issues are being grappled with under the cover of our arguments about homosexuality. For example, I think many people see homosexuality as the front line in a battle between Democrats and Republicans, or socialists and capitalists, or whatever. They're talking "homosexuality" but they're thinking "free enterprise" or "small government." Or they might be arguing about how to interpret the Bible, as I was mentioning a minute ago. Or they might be arguing for a re-emphasis on personal sexual morality, which is a tremendously important issue.

But so far, I haven't seen many people change their views on homosexuality through arguments, one way or the other. What changes their views is when they meet people—really get to know them—who are different. For example, when a "liberal" Christian meets a compassionate person who believes homosexuality is a sin, or when a "conservative" person discovers his daughter or nephew or best friend is gay, that tends to notch the rhetoric up to a higher level, a more human level.

**How do you reconcile the need to affirm orthodoxy without becoming exclusionary snobs?**

*Brian McLaren:* Well, I think we begin by deciding that we need a third alternative that rejects being careless about truth on the one hand, but that also rejects being exclusionary snobs on the other. I think a part of what's going on in these conversations requires us to look at the Bible in some fresh ways. We're not paying less attention to the Bible, but we're realizing that we also need to pay attention to the ways we read or interpret the Bible. We need to go back and uncover our assumptions about how we think the Bible is supposed to function in the Christian community. For example, even though no Christian scholars that I know of support the dictation theory of inspiration—you know, that God dictated the Bible to the biblical writers the way Muslims believe God dictated the Qur'an to Mohammed—I'd have to say that an awful lot of the preaching I hear sounds like it assumes the dictation theory. It's a lot more Qur'anic than incarnational, at least to my ears. And many of us assume that the biblical writers must have written like reporters for the *Wall Street Journal* or *Business Week*. But maybe they were writing more like Anne Lamott writes one of her confessional books, or more like Mary Oliver writes a poem. So maybe we're learning to take the Bible literarily, not just literally, and to respect divine inspiration as an artistic reality more than a journalistic process.

**Why is the emergent church going gangbusters in the UK and this British invasion is just starting to hit the US shores?**

*Brian McLaren:* I can think of two main reasons. First, the UK is one of the premier postcolonial nations in the world, while the United States is just getting its colonial testosterone running in its system. So, the United States is trying to build an empire, but the UK is living in the aftermath of what it means to have an empire. That makes Christians in the US a lot less reflective, a lot more prone to say "Let's just keep doing what we're doing, but doing it more and louder and harder and faster." In places like the UK and across Western and Eastern Europe, they're way beyond that. Second, in the UK, they're generally up to their neck in postmodern philosophy—what you might call a post-Christian culture. I've heard it said that more people go to Ikea in London on a weekend than to church. They're in a different missional situation. Our churches in the US still think they're strong, even though they're stagnant in terms of growth. We don't realize how naked the emperor is yet because we have a lot of money, and political power, and a larger percentage of regular attenders at our services.

### ⬤ N. T. WRIGHT (in person)

**Why has the emerging church been thriving in the UK for years and we're just now starting this dialogue here in the States?**

*N. T. Wright:* If the UK appears to be further ahead regarding the emerging church, it's because the ordinary church has declined further and faster. For example, megachurches aren't heard of in the UK. There are so many people unchurched that emerging church came along and found the door wide open.

**How do we reach people for whom church is not part of their vocabulary?**

*N.T. Wright:* All human beings are made in God's image, and it is this image that is the bridgehead to God. People know this in their bones even if they don't consider themselves to be religious. And let's not forget that church wasn't in people's vocabulary when Christianity first started.

**What does it mean for us to be living in the fifth act: the time of the church?**

> *N.T. Wright:* In *The Last Word*, I explain that we can understand the Bible best if we read it as a five-act play, the five acts being Creation, Fall, Israel, Jesus, and Church. We are not living in an unfallen creation; or in a fallen world without promise; or in the time of Israel BC; or, indeed, in the time of Jesus himself. We are living in the fifth act, and have to improvise, under the guidance of the Spirit, in such a way as to bring this narrative (not some other one!) to its appointed and proper conclusion: in other words, to implement the achievement of Jesus and thus to anticipate the promise of new heavens and new earth.

**Why do we need the Bible?**

> *N.T. Wright:* The Bible is here to equip God's people to carry forward his purposes of new covenant and new creation. It is there to enable people to work for justice, to sustain their spirituality as they do so, to create and enhance relationships at every level, and to produce that new creation that will have something of the beauty of God himself. The Bible isn't like an accurate description of how a car is made. It's more like the mechanic who helps you fix it, the garage attendant who refuels it, and the guide who tells you how to get where you're going. And where you're going is to make God's new creation happen in his world, not simply to find your own way unscathed through the old creation.

**How do we balance the experience of the church with the authority of Scripture?**

> *N.T. Wright:* As we read Scripture, we struggle to understand what God is doing through the world and through us. The phrase "authority of Scripture" can make Christian sense only if it is shorthand for "the authority of the triune God, exercised somehow through Scripture." When we examine what the authority of Scripture means, we're talking about God's authority that is invested in Jesus himself, who says, "All authority in heaven and on earth has been given to me" (Matt 28:18, NRSV).

**This authority phrase is one of the many Scripture quotes that have been misused throughout history by those religious leaders who want to justify their stance on a given sociopolitical position.**

> *N.T. Wright:* In Christian theology, such phrases regularly act as "portable stories"–that is, ways of packing up longer narratives about God, Jesus, the church, and the world, folding them away into convenient suitcases,

and then carrying them about with us. Shorthand enable us to pick up lots of complicated things and carry them around all together. But we should never forget that the point in doing so, like the point of carrying belongings in a suitcase, is that what has been packed away can then be unpacked and put to use in the new location. Too much debate about scriptural authority has had the form of people hitting one another with locked suitcases. It is time to unpack our shorthand doctrines, to lay them out and inspect them. Long years in a suitcase may have made some of the contents go moldy. They will benefit from fresh air, and perhaps a hot iron.

### How do you respond to those who interpret Scripture using the lens of personal experience?

*N.T. Wright:* Experience is a slippery slope philosophically and spiritually. It's a fog in which all sorts of worlds can bump together. Now, no one wants to go to extremes. Some lines are drawn in the sand. For example, no one in their right mind would endorse mass murder. But we need to follow a path of wisdom and have standards. When you come into the life of the church, there is a way of life followed there. There are codes of conduct. It's like when you come into someone's home. You take off your muddy boots when you enter the house. You don't take tea and pour it down someone's back. There are standards in how we live together. Experience needs to be affirmed, redirected, and rebuked by God's authority. Because of our propensity to self-deception, we constantly need to check against Scripture whether we are allowing the word of God's grace in the gospel, and God's reaffirmation of us as made in his image, to validate what is in fact an idolatrous and distorted form of humanness. When, through letting Scripture be the vehicle of God's judging and healing authority in our communities and individual lives, we really do "experience" God's affirmation, then we shall know as we are known.

### How do you account for the intense criticism that appears to be leveled against people like Steve Chalke who got death threats after he published his book *The Lost Message of Jesus*?

*N.T. Wright:* Now, I don't agree with all of his work. But I do know that Steve Chalke read my book on Jesus as part of the preparation for his book on Jesus—because he told me so. The anger you're mentioning stems from the fact that there is an enormous resistance, in post-Reformation circles, to taking seriously the actual meaning and message of

Matthew, Mark, Luke, and John. The Reformers treated them merely as documents from which to cull doctrines and teachings rather than as the God-given account of how Israel's story, and actually God's story, came rushing to their climax. The result is that "substitutionary atonement," which is undoubtedly taught in the New Testament, has been expounded in several different and sometimes hopelessly inadequate and sub-biblical ways. My view of Steve Chalke is that he has attacked some of those inadequate ways without seeing that there might be good, and fully biblical, ways of re-expressing substitution. In addition, he has quite correctly seen that the gospel message of Jesus has enormous political implications. I think some people have taken fright at that and have used his rejection of (some versions of) substitutionary atonement as an excuse to go after him.

# CHAPTER 3

# Hospitality to the Stranger

 STEPHANIE SPELLERS (in person)

**What were the key findings of your Radical Welcome Project?**

*Stephanie Spellers:* Everybody loves the idea of welcoming the Other, the stranger, the marginalized. But in the course of traveling the country, conducting interviews, and studying these communities, I discovered the extent to which you simply must deal with fear, and we don't have a lot of tools for that. If you can't talk honestly about why you're scared to interact with the stranger, then you can't have an open conversation.

The other insight was the degree to which this is not about just doing the right or the nice thing, but it's about hope and a gospel vision. The Radical Welcome Project became a way of writing and talking about our hope and vision for the future, our need to learn how to share power, and so that individuals and congregations will transformed by the presence and power of the Other.

**There are those who will say you need to be in a certain theological relationship with God in order to be accepted into a church community.**

*Stephanie Spellers:* I grew up in the South and was surrounded by conservative evangelical churches. So I don't dismiss those theological perspectives. But I do say that my understanding of the way of Christ is that where some folks would say, "I can't welcome that oppressed person," I have to say, "I'm sorry but Christ is sitting in the life of that person." If the wall can come down, then not only do you embrace the

Other, you can accept the true welcome and grace of Christ—for them and for yourself!

I started my research in earnest in the summer of 2003, at the very time that the General Convention consented to Gene Robinson's election as Bishop of New Hampshire. So, I realized as I was researching this book that I was proposing a way of understanding what it means to be church and including gay and lesbian people. That's got to be there. I can live with you if your theology doesn't support welcoming to gays and lesbians, but you can't try to call yourself radically welcoming.

**How can a white suburban church be radically welcoming to the Other without coming off as patronizing?**

*Stephanie Spellers:* I've seen communities struggle and feel guilty because they don't have any Latinos or African Americans. So they think if they put in some elements from these cultures, then that will attract people. I say build up some relationships with people of color, poor people, young adults, gay and lesbians—whoever your neighbor, the Other, is for you. Reflect on where your own community needs to go so that it can better reflect the life of kingdom of God. I think it has to come from a place of being in relationship with people—outside or inside your congregation—rather than picking through a book and choosing some elements that you feel will appeal to this population.

**Some predominately African American churches are very Anglo-Catholic. From an outsider's perspective, it seems they prefer high church music. So, why change a gathering that appears to be working?**

*Stephanie Spellers:* I've seen a lot of communities say that the black Anglicans coming from the Islands are more Anglo than we [in the United States] are. So, they say, who are we to impose African or Caribbean cultural styles into the worship mix if that's what they want?

The one thing we have to acknowledge here is that, yes, black people can have a preference for something European and yes, that can feel authentic for us. But we also have to talk about the role of colonialism in defining what we prefer, and not use the fallback of, this is the way it's always been. The whole point of colonialism is that the colonizer tells the colonized that our culture isn't really holy. "Put that evil, dirty culture aside. You need this instead." So, I want to sit down with my brothers and sisters from any number of colonial contexts—including some right here in America—and ask them about the music, the images, the movement, the leadership, they experienced at home that lifted their spirits. How do we pull some of those resources in? We've got to break open our whole definition of what's holy and Anglican to include what's found in non-European, younger, working-class and poor and queer cultures.

## How do we deal with the fear that change brings?

*Stephanie Spellers:* Paolo Freire's book *The Pedagogy of the Oppressed* talks about how none of us is free until everybody gets free. Like it or not, liberation has to happen for the oppressor, who is acting out of a place of fear and not liberation. Otherwise, the oppressive system never fundamentally changes. But if this person can be freed from the fear of annihilation, the fear that everything will be taken away from them if the Other gets power and standing, then you can build a different kind of community. Then you discover that, like love, power can grow when it's spread.

This is where my Buddhist background kicks in. I studied Buddhism before I studied Christianity. I embrace the idea of approaching fear—an emotion we thought of as an enemy or demon—just approaching and observing this fear and saying "hi." Explore why this fear exists. Ask yourself, Why am I so afraid? What do I think will happen to the church leadership and the sense of decorum during worship, if the Other is allowed in? Why do I think my voice wouldn't matter anymore? Explore the fear and then maybe you can release the fear and then really welcome this new person and their gifts and know that it doesn't threaten all that you have and all that you are.

## How can we create a culture where clergy can let their guard down enough so this can happen?

*Stephanie Spellers:* Radical transformation requires planting seeds and spreading the catalyzers, the fertilizer. Someone else has to model this new way of being, because most folks have no idea what it even looks like or why they should bother. I honestly think that's one of the roles of a charismatic leader like Bishop Michael Curry (North Carolina) or so many others—it's to paint a picture of this radical community. Everyone nods and says, "Yes! That's what I want!" Then we can introduce the mechanics of how we get there and talk about sacrifice, conversion, and mutual transformation as a gift. But somebody has got to introduce the possibility so that folks realize, there's a cost, but there's something beautiful to gain. There's such a joy and freedom and holiness in this way of being with the Other. God has been speaking in all these

**59**

lives and cultures, and now we can share and learn from each other. Together we can write a new story.

## How do you create a community where the homeless and the bluebloods can call this their church?

*Stephanie Spellers:* There has to be trust among all the people and the change leaders (and I'm not assuming the change leaders are clergy), so that people know something new is being introduced, but they trust they will be held by this community in love no matter who else they invite in from the outside or from the margins. I am convinced, after interviewing all these communities and leaders, that if people know that they are loved, they can walk through a lot together.

## Any final thoughts on creating an atmosphere of radical welcome while maintaining the integrity of a church's tradition?

*Stephanie Spellers:* People need to have consensus and we do need to point as to what is bona fide Anglican. We're not just throwing out the baby with the bathwater and grabbing every trend that comes our way. The next book I want to write is something like *You Call That Anglican?* I want to talk to some of these folks that I call "edge riders," about how is what you're doing Episcopalian? Karen Ward has one of the most wonderful explanations of what she does. She talks about the gems of the tradition, the emphasis on spiritual practice, gathering, the incarnation. Lots of us have identified what's essential, and what we love and desperately want to see survive for more generations. But right now, the traditional Episcopal liturgy speaks from a very white, educated, monied, owning-class cultural context. If that's the only way of self-expression that we have, the only thing that can receive the label "authentically Episcopalian," then the church deserves to be marginalized and to shrink away.

## ✉ KURT NEILSON (e-mail)

## How do you define "hospitality"?

*Kurt Neilson:* "Hospitality" is openness to the Other, recognizing as we do the Other in ourselves. We are all in need of utter hospitality: we are all broken, in need of home and safety, in need of the healing welcome of God. To be hospitable is to recognize in ourselves this need and to seek to respond to it by welcoming in humility the brokenness of others. Essential to this journey is putting aside an assumption that we "know" the unique journey of the Other (this helps to rescue us from condescending "philanthropy" or misguided do-gooding). Listening, listening is essential.

**How can churches help enable members of their congregation to reach outside their comfort zone and embrace the stranger?**

*Kurt Neilson:* Oh, oh my. I think it takes a long, long time, a long time of explicating the "whole Gospel," over and over, explicating the radical and countercultural nature of the proclamation of the reign of God, combined with pushing into practice concrete outreach projects and experiences of engaging the Other and listening. It is a genuine conversion of the heart—not the instantaneous revival-style moment of conversion (although some folks who experience such regard that moment as the beginning of their journey into openness to the Other), but more in the sense of "conversio" of Saint Benedict: daily, ongoing opening of the heart and spirit based on community experience of service and openness to the Spirit of God.

**How do you create a welcoming church?**

*Kurt Neilson:* I was fortunate in that Saints Peter and Paul already had an unassuming, down-to-earth working-class culture and a tradition of offering a Wednesday night meal that had people accustomed to seeing the poor come in and out. We broadened the leadership and participation-base of the meal to include as many as a third of the active congregation at any one time, exposed newcomers especially to the meal (now called "Brigid's Table" in honor of St. Brigid of Kildare) as an incorporation piece, and finally offered the Celtic Christian monastic model as a new way of envisioning parish community. Part of this model is the sense of "porous boundaries" that welcomes pilgrims and the poor into the circle.

✉ KESTER BREWIN (e-mail)

**How do you define hospitality to the stranger?**

*Kester Brewin:* With difficulty. Jesus was asked "so who is my neighbour" and gave the parable of the Good Samaritan. That was a clear case of hospitality. Now, with our interactions/relationships so broken up and fragmented, it can be less easy to work that out. If I share a bottle of wine with my next-door-neighbour, am I being hospitable? Am I only being hospitable if the wine is fairly traded? We have the potential to encounter thousands of strangers on the way to work each day in London. How do we show hospitality to them? Is it possible to? Who is most needy? Is it the guy begging for money, or successful guy in the suit who is desperately lonely?

So perhaps we are just left with this: hospitality to the stranger is less about actively finding that "other" than making sure that I am actively opening myself to the awareness of who among these crowds might need that hospitable moment.

**How do you minister to those for whom church is not in their vocabulary?**

*Kester Brewin:* I guess that answer is obvious—without words! Trouble is, church is in everyone's vocabulary. But for too many it's a word that carries far too much negative meaning. So we minister to them without using the words.

**What outreach strategies have you found to be effective in an urban environment versus those methods that tend to further alienate those for whom church is not a part of their vocabulary?**

*Kester Brewin:* Creative and artistic stuff. If I'm right about the city, the city is all about co-creating with God. . . . In the buildings, the galleries, the concert halls we see humanity and divinity working together. So if you emphasise the creative, you naturally draw people toward the creator.

**What criticisms have you gotten for working with those considered to be on the fringes of society, and how do you address these concerns?**

*Kester Brewin:* Been accused of 'backsliding' a few times, but apart from that haven't had much criticism.

**Elaborate on this statement—"The city started life as a statement of independence from God but ended up through Christ as presenting perfectly the goal of divine and human cohabitation."**

*Kester Brewin:* We have neglected to reflect on the importance of the city, and ignored the biblical metaphor of the city, and thus ended up neglecting the cities we (used to) live in. We've demonised them, in other words.

## ✉ PATRICIA HENDRICKS (e-mail)

*Patricia Hendricks:* Hospitality means welcoming all, without distinction, to an atmosphere that is warm and to a people who are happy to worship in this place. It takes courage for most people to enter the door of a church for the first time, and it is wise for those who belong to that church to ponder this question: Why are new people coming here? Some people are coming with hurts caused by attendance in other churches. Some haven't been to a church in a long time while others have never belonged to a congregation. Some come because they are troubled or lonely. Others enter the door of a church because they are hungry for a God who is real and vital.

In my visits with churches over the past five years, the ones who were most faithful in welcoming people were the emergent ones. In all cases, the setting was informal either in a room or a sanctuary that felt informal. There were usually simple decorations, candles and holy objects or natural objects. People were stationed at the doors to welcome folks. They introduced themselves and engaged in small talk. Nametags were used for all. Often there were refreshments before, after and during the service. People of all ages attended, and those who were younger were given major roles. People were honest about their faith and did not hide their struggles with life.

Being a companion to young people is to openly show respect for them. In a church setting, the smallest gestures are meaningful. Smiling at children or commenting on what they are wearing or what they brought to church. Saying "hi" to a teen—especially the one with the bare-midriff or the tattoo or the multi-pierced ear. Showing respect includes the attitude that I can learn from you, and whether you are three or twenty-six, you have something to contribute to this church.

Companioning young people also includes honesty. We are free to admit that we don't have answers, that we, too, have questions. Yet we have been "down the road" a little farther and can offer encouragement and a listening ear.

This is why intergenerational relationships are so important. Younger folks need to be invited to serve on the church council and to work repairing homes—not just as a youth group project but as a church wide project. Pounding nails, painting walls, and voting on church issues create opportunities for mutual respect and appreciation. The church I attend has its annual meeting in January. Those who are sixteen and older attend one meeting. Those three to fifteen conduct their own annual meeting in another part of the building. After the adult meeting is over, the younger people of the church join us to share their reflections and suggestions on the state of the church.

I have seen a handful of churches that have been faithful in reaching out to the twenty and thirty something generation. Those churches typically have these qualities:

1. Sunday service that is spiritually and intellectually challenging and that invites people to experience the presence of God.

2. An invitation to take part in the life and work of the congregation when the newcomer is ready.

3. A clear statement that all are welcome in the congregation.

4. A balance between seriousness and playfulness.

### NANCY HANNA (in person)

**How does Calvary/St. George interact with the various parachurch organizations that meet at these churches?**

*Nancy Hanna:* The Haven, a group of local artists, meets on Monday night and we give them free space. It's a gift of this parish to support young Christian artists. They're part of Priority Associates, which is a ministry of Campus Crusade for Christ. We also have a partnership with Young Life. Their New York regional office is at St. George's—their work is mostly with newly immigrant kids. We haven't figured out how to get those kids into our Sunday worship life. So, I see us giving them space as more of a ministry to them. What is a more effective church partnership is with Fellowship of Christians at Universities and Schools (FOCUS). It's now run by a member of our congregation. A number of our middle age kids go to FOCUS gatherings.

**What advice would you give to churches who are considering forming partnerships with parachurch organizations or an individual who wants to start a ministry?**

*Nancy Hanna:* We rent to other Christian groups, but they are separate entities. They bring us income. That's all. I don't think we expect to see cross ministry with these groups. My goal would be to do less of that and more of our own ministry using the space for worship and gatherings of other kinds. I think you need to plant and grow from within because the theology needs to be theology with integrity. We tend to be evangelical Anglicans here so when we decided to offer a Sunday night service and attract new people, we decided to do it from within. I've observed how it has been a problem bringing someone in from the outside to help launch a new ministry.

For example, in addition to The Haven, we have another artists group that includes some of members of our vestry. What we say to people who come to us wanting to start an artists' group is to come worship with us at one of our Sunday services. And we'll try to help you to do what you want to do.

**How do you see the Internet as a tool to welcome the stranger?**

*Nancy Hanna:* The Internet can connect people's hearts and minds by breaking down miles and walls. We know couples who met on the Internet who exchange each other's minds and hearts and then physical reality followed. There's a new way to define church in that people can get together for Bible study and comment about something with one another without having to physically come together. On the other hand, as Christians we have an understanding of incarnation. God chose to speak to us ultimately in person, in flesh and blood and that's not an accident. Therefore ultimately any church must connect people in their flesh and blood. The wafer is put in people's hands and the cup is put to their lips—that's very Christian and very profound.

# CHAPTER 4

# Forming Christian Community

 ISAAC EVERETT (in person)

**How do you define community?**

*Isaac Everett:* My church was a place where I had adult friends who were not my parents. It was where I learned to take care of toddlers. It was the place where the people who heard me play piano when I was five years old also came to my senior recital. A church is one step larger than a family. In America, a church community fulfills the same function that an extended family does in traditional societies.

**What was the genesis behind forming Transmission?**

*Isaac Everett:* I turned to Bowie Snodgrass one day and said, "Let's start a church." She went, "OK," and that was that. Transmission was founded partly because I wasn't finding a community that worked for me and partly because I knew a lot of other people who were interested in Christianity but turned off by traditional church. I also knew a lot of church professionals who weren't fully integrated into the communities they were serving—it's difficult, as it should be, to both an employee and a full community member.

So we decided to get all these people together and form Transmission. We decided that starting an alternative worship service simply wasn't enough—there are plenty of traditional churches in New York City offering "cool worship," but I wasn't hungry for one more event to attend. I was hungry for a life lived in real community.

**Explain how you came up with the name for your community.**

*Isaac Everett:* Well, Transmission is who we are, but it's also what we do. Sometimes we call our gatherings "rituals," sometimes we call them "services," but most often we call them "transmissions." A transmission is "the act of passing something on," and this reminds us to make worship active, engaging, and participatory. Tom Driver makes the case that "in a Christian sacrament the way of God's becoming present to us is for one human being to become radically present to another. The mysterious One who is sacramentally present in worship is not one but two—both the neighbor and God." We take this seriously and strive to encounter and engage each other a consistent part of worship. We don't just transmit to each other, however—we all see ourselves in continuity with the Christian tradition that has been transmitted through history. As Paul says, "I transmitted (*paradosis*) to you as of first importance what I in turn had received," which is very important because good communication is at the heart of good relationships.

There are a bunch of other reasons why the name "Transmission" fits us. First, the word "mission" is embedded in Transmission, and having a mission is one of the things that distinguishes a community of faith from a social club. Second, the prefix "trans" calls to mind our commitment to the sexually marginalized—the transgendered community is the cutting edge of society's struggle with sexual identity, and we feel a call to be in relationship with that community. Finally, a transmission is a car part. It helps you change gears. It gets you up the hill.

**Why do you feel the need to form a church plant outside the structure of the Episcopal Church?**

*Isaac Everett:* I love the Episcopal Church and it's been very formative for me over the years, but I'm not entirely comfortable with the hierarchical structures of authority and the way those power dynamics affect the church's culture. Liturgy tends to be very clergy-centric, and the laity are mostly passive during worship. A lot of people out there have become so distrustful of institutions that they have no desire to sit quietly in a pew and listen to an elite authority figure define truth for them. We don't trust the government, we don't trust corporations—why should we trust the church?

The vision of the kingdom that we're given in the New Testament has no rich, no poor, no Jew, no Greek. There's no "in crowd" in Jesus' vision. Our worship ought to be a witness to that vision, and yet the majority of churches, Episcopal and otherwise, have very hierarchical services. I firmly believe that the mutuality present in a Transmission service comes closer to Jesus' vision of a new society (*basilea*) in which all people are valued.

## What then is the role of clergy?

*Isaac Everett:* When any group gets large enough, at some point it becomes advantageous to say, "It would be tremendously beneficial to us if we had one person whose full-time job is formation of this community." For a community of faith, that's when clergy come into the question. It should be a matter of function, though, not of special authority or apostolic succession. Hiring a clergyperson in this way is not too different from saying, "The bathroom needs to be cleaned so we need to hire a sexton." Having clergy can be a real blessing if they understand their role to be functional, but clergy are often given a sense of authority, entitlement, and empowerment. In the Episcopal Church, lay people are often uncomfortable having a Bible study or a small group without a priest present, let along having communion.

Transmission could work in an Episcopal church if you had a priest who was willing to say, "There's nothing magical about me, I just happen to be a priest." You also need a bishop willing to be hands off. The traditional church's authority is built from the top down, but the new kingdom I see in Christ has authority built from the bottom up.

A whole lot of what makes Transmission meaningful to me is that instead of clergy, we all take turns planning worship, cooking food, and hosting services in our homes. Although worship at Transmission doesn't always reflect my personal preferences, it is always a genuine expression of the community. I'd much rather be part of a community that is willing to take risks than one that is tightly controlled and well-polished.

## What is Transmission doing to ensure accountability as you expand?

*Isaac Everett:* That's a little bit too early for us; we don't even have a budget yet. Since Transmission's expenses get paid out of our pockets, we aren't too concerned with financial accountability. We're mostly young, broke artist-types, so we get pretty creative about doing services on the cheap. It's working for us right now, but as the community gets bigger, it's something we'll have to think about. We don't have a magical solution, or even a plan.

There is a limit to how large a free-form community like ours can be. If Transmission ever got larger than fifty people, it would become a very different community. For one, we'd need more rigid structures of governance. If we ever get there, maybe we'll split the group in half and have two Transmissions. Eventually, we could have hundreds of these small, intimate communities all in relationship with one another.

## How do you respond to those who say you are holy hipsters?

*Isaac Everett:* Being a Christian should be decidedly uncool; it's not cool to go without a lot of money, it's not cool to value compassion over power, and it's not cool to hold back snarky gossip, but those are all the things that Christ taught us to do. If we spend too much time trying to become cool, than the kingdom of God becomes indistinguishable from the kingdom of earth. As Shane Claiborne says, God wants us to be hot or cold, but not cool.

Isaac Everett as quoted in "Is Casual the New Christian?" The Ooze, August 8, 2007 (www.theooze.com)

## ♦ SHANE CLAIBORNE (in person)

## What was your take on interning at Willow Creek?

*Shane Claiborne:* One of the things I remember hearing at Willow Creek is (that) you reproduce who you are for better or worse. I'm really careful not to reproduce the Simple Way because I know all our goofiness and we want people to try to figure out community but not copycat what we're doing.

## Seems every megachurch is modeled after Willow Creek, though.

*Shane Claiborne:* I think the problem with folks kind of copycatting Willow Creek is they began where Willow Creek has ended up. So you end up copying the drums and drama but not the disenchantment with the church that gave birth to Willow Creek. They started out a bunch of teenagers that were pretty ticked off with the church and went door-to-door selling tomatoes and getting to know their neighbors. So if you want to follow the Willow Creek model, I'd say go door-to-door selling tomatoes and get to know your neighbors.

## They're selling a lot more than tomatoes these days.

*Shane Claiborne:* Bill Hybels and I wrestled ten years over this $50 million building project. I was encouraging them to do a Jubilee Campaign so they would redistribute as much money as they were putting into the building.

**Why do you think so many churches can't be as all-inclusive as Jesus was?**

*Shane Claiborne:* What I've seen is a self-righteousness that we've got it all together on both sides. It's, "Thank you that we're not like people that listen to secular music or are homosexuals" or, on the other side it's, "Thank you that we're not like those people that don't eat organic or are Bush lovers." I see a lot of hope, though, because I think there are a lot of younger folks that are marked by humility, and postmodernity gives a chance to sort of go, "Hey, we don't really fit into any of those categories."

**So the desire is to fuse the best of the old with the best of the new, and then create something else?**

*Shane Claiborne:* I think what we settle for a lot of the time is contextualization of the medium so we use the matrix, candles, and all these things. But the real hope is that we can begin to see the life of the Scriptures inform what it means to live in the middle of our culture and our empire. I think a lot of people are starting to talk about this in a healthy way.

**Seems there is a longing for Jesus and people don't know quite what to do with it.**

*Shane Claiborne:* Yes, it's a good longing. I really think that the courage a lot of folks have to speak out in those areas and to actually be a voice that reconciles attracts the kind of people that Jesus attracted.

**So, are you guys just some hippie freaks?**

*Shane Claiborne:* I think with the Jesus Movement there was this sort of pretension that we're going to do church better than other people are. We see our discontent with the church is the very reason that we engage rather than pull out. Within the brokenness of the church is our own brokenness. That's why we are active in local congregations.

**On a practical note, how does this community of six to ten members work? You've got to pay rent, electricity, food, and so on.**

*Shane Claiborne:* Our community has layers. A few of us are partners, a few are novices like one to two years, then guests for three months, and then visitors and supporters. While we get a lot of donations for stuff like school supplies, we pay our bills by working part-time jobs. The reason we work part-time jobs is because of all the stuff we do in the neighborhoods.

**How do you respond when people ask if you're a cult?**

> *Shane Claiborne:* Cult comes from the same word as culture or cultivate, and we are kind of like cultivating a different environment. So that's why we do crazy things, like we don't watch TV, or we have times when we pray together or sing together. People aren't just attracted to the Simple Way, but they're very attracted to an alternative culture that's not even just countercultural, but it sort of has imagination and alternatives for this fragile world our parents have left us.

## ☎ PETER ROLLINS (phone)

**One of the major complaints about independent church plants is the lack of accountability.**

> *Peter Rollins:* On a structural level, we try to avoid this problem by maintaining good relationships with local churches in the area that allow them to speak into our group. While at an individual level, we try to encourage each other that our decisions about stuff like where we live, what we eat, what kind of car we drive, etc. are not private decisions but ones that have an impact beyond our private lives. As such we try to encourage each other to talk to others about these matters and engage in two-way relational accountability, rather than some one-way hierarchical accountability.
>
> In a sense at Ikon, we try to make sure that one person does not have too much power. For instance, the people around me are committed to making sure that I don't try to take too much power. You can think of Ikon like a donut. There's the jam donut where all the good stuff is centered in the middle. But we're more like a donut with a hole in it. The people who organize Ikon are not some sort of center. Instead, we engage in relational pasturing and relational tithing rather than seeking our pastoral support from the center or giving our money to the center.

## ♦ KEVIN BEAN (in person)

**How do you define church growth?**

> *Kevin Bean:* There are seven or eight what we and others would call universals for growth. These are applicable to any parish of any size and any denomination in any geographical location. For example, every church has worship but is that worship inspiring? We're not only about creating disciples but also welcoming seekers for whom church has not

been in their vocabulary. So, we've created worship that's not only inspiring but done so in a way that creates diversity by offering services with different styles at various times.

Another universal is relationships. Every church has relationships, but are they loving? Is there a mutually caring environment? This goes into the third universal—the church has small groups, but are they nurturing, caring, and loving? Fourthly, every church has a spirituality, but is there a passionate and diverse spirituality going on? Fifth, every church has ministries, but are they gift oriented? In other words, a lot of churches look for the next person in their door and try to turn them into worker bees. But if you approach people to help them discover what they are gifted with and where their passion is and calling might be, then you're going to get a very different way of people claiming their ministry. One of our popular courses here is called "What in God's Name Are You Doing?"

Sixth, every church has administrative structures, but are they flexible, porous, and transparent? This is a large church, and it can be kind of daunting for people. We talk about having a radical welcome here, but once people are welcomed, it can feel like radical confusion. We've worked hard to enable people to understand how staff works and how they can be at the service of the ministry of the people and not the other way.

Seventh, every church has leadership, but is it empowering? A lot of smaller churches operate on the pretense that the clergy person at the center can only have about 150 relationships. Many churches never expand beyond this because they can't operate on a model of shared leadership.

Finally, every church has some form of outreach; the question is whether that outreach is fully engaging of the wider community and the congregation itself. Does the outreach take you where you need to go to join Christ's mission of repairing the world? Most churches are most comfortable with the charity model where people who have resources give to people who do not. But there are other models—in advocacy, organizing, and community development—that draw out the full potentials of church members while truly serving the common good. Attentiveness to all these tends toward growth. The churches that don't pay attention to these universals tend not to grow.

**How do you engage in outreach without becoming a political pawn?**

*Kevin Bean:* Anything that is true to the gospel will also be socially responsible. Spiritual renewal and social responsibility go together hand in hand. They are two sides of the same coin. The type of work that the church can engage in that is being true to its call will be political in the Greek (*polis*) sense of the word, thus connecting to the public arena. So we are political, but not partisan. We're value driven but not ideological. We are civil but not soft. And we are involved, but we are not used or co-opted by other forces, be they governmental or commercial. There are a lot of churches unfortunately that get co-opted. It's important for churches to find their voice and act maturely. We seek that right balance that has us being the responsible church in the world.

**How does a church know if they are truly welcoming people?**

*Kevin Bean:* People are seeking before they get into a church. There is some issue or transition in their lives that sets people in a search mode. If they have a searching itch, we need to be able to give them a little scratch. They're testing and if a church is a one size fits all kind of a thing, they don't see diverse options. We need to provide various ways to enter that allow them to enter at a stage or pace that each person is able to accept. You never get a second chance to make a first impression.

We need to make the ministry of welcome accountable, both in terms of taking the newcomer into account, and in terms of measuring the effectiveness of our approaches. Are we seeing people coming back, and are we helping them to go deeper? Are we inviting them to join in? This church is not just about filling the pews with people but is also about how we help the seeker become a disciple? So that involves us offering a number of seeker friendly courses that are short and often repeated, as well as numerous other opportunities to find meaning, purpose, and community.

There are many "doors" into any church, even a small church. People just need to know what those doors are. These doors should be opened wide. Yes, there's the Sunday door, but there's, for example, an additional children's entrance as it were for families. The children, youth, and family ministries are where St. Bart's right now is experiencing our greatest growth.

**Given that you have such a diverse range of services that attract different communities, how do you bring the entire church community together?**

*Kevin Bean:* We do some larger worship, fellowship, educational, music, and outreach events throughout the year. There's also an oscillation where people are happy with one service or Bible study or small group, but sometimes they check out other liturgies and opportunities.

**How do you know when you need to enact change within a community? For example, you came in and completely redesigned the Sunday night "Come as You Are" service even though others were happy with the current folk mass.**

*Kevin Bean:* Some services have a certain lifespan and after a while they get stale. The 7 p.m. service had unknowingly erected passive barriers to growth by the way the music was sung and the way the space was set up, and the way the "radical welcome" had turned inward on itself. We were watching this over time, and we knew we had to reinvent the experience so it could invite others.

Also, the whole way these services develop is through this radical welcome and building of community. You need to do something when you begin to see that people's attention is not being spent on the next person who could come through the door but talking with their friends. To paraphrase William Temple, "The church exists primarily not for its own members." That doesn't mean you neglect the people who are in the church. It's important to develop leadership and strengthen the ties that bind people.

**What did you learn from having to go through this change that you feel will be helpful to other churches that are in a situation where they have to make a change that is deemed unpopular?**

*Kevin Bean:* Change creates an anxiety, and the key to this is to be leaders who aren't so anxious themselves—for that anxiety only creates more of the same in others. That is not an easy thing to do. You also show regard for people. We spent hours with people, who were upset and felt they were being excluded from the decision. We took these relationships seriously. That doesn't mean everyone ended up happy, and there has been some back and forth with some people leaving the church.

**You hired an outside consultant to help design the new Sunday night service titled "Emerge." What are the pluses and minuses to this approach?**

*Kevin Bean:* For whatever reason, this particular consultant wasn't helping with some of the important research and development work that needed to happen. Then that person also got very passive when it came time to develop and roll out the liturgy. So it ended up being 99 percent of our own work anyway. What we realized was that some of our best assets are right here in the church—the architecture, the lighting, the candles, the ability to create a contemplative space, not to mention our human resources, both volunteer and staff. Our previous service could have been held in a church auditorium. A key question to ask when doing any change is what are the best practices out there? Who can we beg, borrow, and steal from—and acknowledge—their help? So we did quite a bit of research on other practices of other emergent church liturgies.

**For a church with limited resources, when would you suggest hiring an outside consultant?**

*Kevin Bean:* In my last parish, which is about a fourth the size of St. Bart's, we hired Alice Mann from Alban Institute to help us with a roadmap for growth. That church had kept making the same mistakes over and over again—it would grow and but then make bad decisions and then plateau. Plateaus are never good. It's a sign that there's an active or passive barrier to growth. If you leave the plateau alone, it will start to decline. Alice helped us get out of that bad cycle, so we could do some more intentional things to invest in ways we needed to for growth. And we grew. In fact, her book, *The In-Between Church: Navigating Size Transitions in Congregations* (Alban Institute, 1998) uses that parish as a guinea pig for such a navigation exercise in growth; although she changed the name of the parish to "protect the innocent."

**How does the Center for Religious Inquiry help to create community?**

*Kevin Bean:* This is a very interesting interfaith door into St. Bart's, led by a progressive rabbi on our staff. We have people in the congregation and from the wider cosmopolitan region of New York who are seeking to learn and grow from the vitality of several faith traditions. We are able to provide courses that help people go deeper in their intellectual and spiritual quest. Now, we do this with a kind of confidence that is also a kind of paradox. If you belong to Christ, you belong to no one else; but because you belong to Christ, you belong to everyone else. Fundamentally, Jesus came to build the bonds of our common humanity. That doesn't mean we don't have a center for our faith. What we like to say is that we are soft around the edges but solid in the center. We know who we are and our center is in Christ. This allows us to take a seat at a table with these other faith traditions. In a similar manner Bishop Krister Stendahl talks about having a "holy envy" of other faith traditions. Even some forms of atheism present a healthy skepticism and a seriousness about human responsibility that we should explore/envy.

## ● ELIZABETH GARNSEY (in person)

**Describe the worship planning that went into preparing to launch your emerging service titled "Emerge."**

> *Elizabeth Garnsey:* About a year and a half ago, we put together a creative team of people, who were hungry for this kind of an experience, to begin planning and talking. A lot of people presented themselves as wanting to work on this. The liturgy came out of exploring the music that we wanted to be urban and authentic while bringing out the best of our tradition. We didn't want any one single sound to define the service. Our music was a constant work in progress. We tried to invent a new sound—atmospheric, meditative, energetic. A sound that people could participate in by singing, but also something meditative, the way Taize allows for a "spacious" meditative participation (i.e., you don't need to depend on a leaflet). We didn't quite hit the mark on this before the service was suspended, but that was our aim.

**How did you see the theme "where the ancient meets the urban come together" being implemented in this service?**

> *Elizabeth Garnsey:* We sought to explore where the ancient and the traditional find urban relevance. People living urban lives connect with tradition and the ancient richness of our faith and they become part of something that's bigger. We found that a receptivity to experiential worship cuts through every demographic, and we have been surprised by the wide range of people who are attracted to this type of service.

**What resources did you find to be the most helpful in planning this service?**

> *Elizabeth Garnsey:* We're a very sacramental church, so it was a given that we were going to have a Eucharist. We used Eucharistic prayers from *Enriching Our Worship*, an authorized Episcopal resource, as well as *Common Worship 2000* (from the Church of England), and we wrote prayers that addressed specific needs of the city and the world and a variety of affirmations of faith other than the Nicene Creed. Other resources we used included music from Iona, Taize, our own *Voices Found*, a hymnal of songs composed and written by women, and Jonny Baker.

**How did you incorporate silence into your service?**

> *Elizabeth Garnsey:* We wanted this to be a place to simply "be." Fifteen minutes before the service began, we'd start with meditative music so

people could settle without any preservice chatter. We'd welcome people at 7 p.m. when the service started. Then we had at least two minutes of silence after the Psalm and the homily. Also, we had prayer desks during communion at all of our services where people could go for quiet prayers and healing.

### Why did St. Bart's close down Emerge?

*Elizabeth Garnsey:* We are suspending this for budgetary restraints. It hasn't been a full year for Emerge so we'll suspend it, but I'm hoping we'll bring it back someday. I think it was a great success. I was thrilled at the response and where we were by the time the service was brought to an untimely end. We had clearly come a long way.

### Given that Emerge is now dark, what lessons did you learn from launching this new service?

*Elizabeth Garnsey:* Emerge began immediately after we brought another service to an end—one that had been running for more than five years, and we wanted to try something new. In hindsight we should have had a simple stripped down Eucharist and then launched the new service instead of imposing a new thing on the heels of the old. There were hurt feelings from people who still enjoyed the old service, and we didn't handle the transition very deftly. Also, we did a lot of silly things in the beginning like vesting acolytes in black vestments that were dark, somber, and, I felt, sinister. There were a lot of elements we experimented with that fell flat, but it was a good learning experience to take risks and be open to change from one week to the next. Also, working with our space has been very difficult to get the feel just right—where to put the altar and put people around it given we have pews and other constraints. We would work on those issues if we bring the service back.

### Any additional advice you would you offer to other churches looking to develop a service such as Emerge?

*Elizabeth Garnsey:* It's important to cultivate a broad team of people in the church willing to publicize and contribute to the creative process. Our steering committee wasn't closed to anybody. We wanted to gather a group of people who have a real heart for this kind of ministry, and very creative energy. My advice to anyone would be to broaden your circle of help and get a team that's willing to collaborate and be faithful. But someone has to be the leader, one who can help keep everyone focused on the main aims and intended tone of the service. Also, we hired a consultant because we had a lack of confidence in our own ideas, but it didn't take long before we realized we had the resources ourselves. Yes, you need to hire some staff, such as talented musicians, but I believe a worship service needs to grow out of the local congregation in order to be the most authentic.

## NANCY HANNA (in person)

### How did Alpha came over to the United States from the United Kingdom?

*Nancy Hanna:* Alpha didn't begin with the idea of becoming a big international thing. A young curate simply hosted a few people in his apartment. They did not start publishing their material until 1992 but people, who attended the Alpha courses in London, were bringing back Xeroxed copies of the material. We got involved in January 1995 when we lived in London while I was on sabbatical. When we attended Holy Trinity Brompton, we heard testimonies by graduates of Alpha. Back then I was head of the Evangelism Committee for the Diocese of New York. So, I was working at Oxford on exploring this topic. I asked Alister McGrath, an amazing Reformation scholar and evangelical Anglican, what he thought of the Alpha course. He said it's not perfect, but it's the best tool there is. In June of 1995, my husband and I attended a two-day Alpha training conference at Holy Trinity Brompton. We turned to each other and said, we're going to do this when we get home. We just heard a recipe that we knew was good.

So we started an Alpha course in our home a few times. Then I was called by Bill Tully to come to St. Bart's in the fall of '96 to run Alpha. Independently of that, I had gone to over London and asked if Nicky Gumbel and Sandy Miller would come and teach a two-day Alpha conference in New York City. About 600 clergy from all over the country attended this conference. A lot of the early Alpha courses started out of this conference. During my 8 years at St. Bart's, we saw about 1,200 to 1,500 people go through the course and about 900 of those stuck around St. Bart's and did something else. In the end, about 600 became pledging members.

### How does Alpha create Christian community in church?

*Nancy Hanna:* First of all, friends bring friends. We have walk-ins, as someone can pick up a brochure in a lobby. Also, at the end of every Alpha course, there's a celebration party where the graduates bring people to that party. At that party, they hear an Alpha talk and get a taste of what Alpha is like.

Many people who have had a religious experience have been hurt or bored tears. They're expecting to be hurt again. So in Alpha, the whole ethos is that the guest feels like they're at a dinner party. Once they get to an Alpha course, it's very key that people sit down around a table with some food no matter how poor you are or what time of day it is.

The heart and soul of Alpha is discussion time after the talk, preferably around a round table. It's very simple and true that people begin to relate to each other around table. We train table hosts to host guests— we don't use the words teacher and student. It's all about getting to know the guests and avoiding anything religious. That's a social time. We choose hosts who are people people and good listeners.

Over and over again, we've heard people say I've never been at a church where I could say this and not be argued. It's finding a place where people are received and not judged. My experience has been that Alpha grads feel that they've been heard and they want to share that with others and welcome them in.

As part of this ten-week course, there's also the weekend away in which about 50 percent of the people enrolled in the course chose to go. Often people who have chosen to go away on the weekend are open enough to the whole idea of God to where they're open to being touched by the Holy Spirit. Alpha is designed to lead people to having a personal relationship in Jesus Christ.

Alpha exists in a local congregation to be a place where they can bring unchurched people in to make evangelism easy. It's meant so every member of that congregation can bring a friend in to a dinner, where they can be exposed to good biblical teachings and the basics of Christianity in a way that's exciting and fun. So it's all about building up the local church, which I think is the New Testament model for church growth.

### Can you elaborate on the ecumenical nature of Alpha?

*Nancy Hanna:* It's being used by every possible denomination. It's really growing in the Roman Catholic churches. My husband left his position with Alpha USA two years ago and is working to bring Alpha to Central and South America.

Alpha is now in pubs and prisons all over the world. Church is probably the worst place to run Alpha. Any out of church traditional space helps people who are unchurched.

**How do you respond to those who criticize Alpha for being too "conservative?"**

*Nancy Hanna:* Conservative is a totally meaningless word these days. Alpha teaches the doctrine of substitutionary atonement, and I've heard some people say they don't believe that anymore. I think this is crucial to the heart and soul of the gospel and it's what changes lives.

There were many gay Alpha leaders when I was at St. Bart's. There's one sentence in the Alpha curriculum where Nicky talks about sex outside of marriage. "The biblical context of sex is the lifelong commitment of a man and a woman in marriage." Now, when I was at St. Bart's, I didn't read the first sentence because I didn't want to offend the gays and lesbians there. But when I talked about the course's teachings against casual sex, everyone nodded their head in agreement. Interested parties in this topic can read Nicky Gumbel's pamphlet, "What is the Christian Attitude Toward Homosexuality?" I think what people are really opposed to, though, is the doctrine of substitutionary atonement and this is the red herring.

**How can a church plug into the Alpha program?**

*Nancy Hanna:* Worship leaders who would like to bring Alpha to their congregation, can go to the website (www.alphausa.org) and enroll in the nearest two-day Alpha training course.

## SPENCER BURKE:
Moving beyond Megachurch

☎ SPENCER BURKE, creator of The Ooze (www.theooze.com)
(via phone)

*Spencer Burke:* I set out to be a teaching pastor in a nondenominational church in Southern California with ten thousand members or more. It took me twenty-two years, but I got there. My friend Richard Rohr said you spend the first thirty-five years of your life building your tower and then you jump off. Every book, class, article said you want to get here and I got there, and in many ways, it wasn't worth achieving.

I think we set out to be ministers to love those whom Christ loved, to reach out to those who many times cannot find God. In that sense, I would say that I was a minister because I loved Jesus. As I became more successful, I became an administrator to the point where you had to get to me via my secretary. Within the church institution, I really did shoot for the top and got into that top 1 percent of the game.

In the '80s, megachurches were boastful because the mainline churches were in decline. We were the fastest growing Christian phenomenon around and we were thinking we were doing the word of God as we were decreasing. We now have a wider view on that statistic, and if you see the total number of people attending church, there was a transfer group of people moving from mainline to a nondenominational megachurch.

When I left Mariners, I said, "Maybe I can't be a paid pastor." At Mariners, we had just started a new church ROCKHarbor—a church plant started at Mariners. I went over there as a volunteer. Before I knew it, I was chair of the board of elders. Then the founding pastor committed adultery and lied about it, so we had to go through a three-year transformation.

We asked what was that one single decision that we made that turned this church into our parents' church? I realized, it wasn't a decision but rather the system it was built on. The second question was we were about to embark on a large church building campaign, and I'm thinking about building another megachurch in Orange County in light of AIDS and other pressing issues. I ended up voting for what was best for the system. When I rotated off my term, we decided to move into a more organic system. Every time that I have moved to the next step in my spiritual journey with my family, it's been a beautiful celebration of what God has done. I still am invited to speak in the pulpits where I've once served.

The Ooze got off the ground back in 1998. We started this website and a social network to talk about what church meant through message boards and articles. It was intended to be a safe place to have a conversation. Now it's grown to where we get over a quarter million people are going to The Ooze each month. It's been this great and wonderful journey of learning together.

**So, how do you define community?**

*Spencer Burke:* When I left Rock Harbor we got together with four other couples. Here I was thinking more in a Netflix mentality or metaphor. Netflix can find out how and why people are doing things, but movies are delivered to your home. If you just bring a church to the home, you just move the institution with you. Churches of communities of forty-nine people and less are growing by leaps and bounds as are the churches of over two thousand people as well.

I've been working on this interesting metaphor along the lines of a Blockbuster total access pass. You can use all the online tools a.k.a. Netflix, but you can also go in person to the Blockbuster store. What if we can do a total access package for church? What if the social networking of all these smaller groups and communities in your area and region can work together and that is church for them? These groups can serve and facilitate the equipping the saints, but then regionally may be three or four churches that may act as the Blockbuster store in a sense. I'm starting to meet with the larger progressive churches in Orange County to see how they can be a regional resource for the smaller communities. The larger regional center can acknowledge that some people are ministered in the smaller communities. Then how do we get these smaller communities to realize that the larger churches aren't trying to steal ministries but work within the context of the offerings available to the regional churches? This could blossom into a fascinating place. We're hooking with all of the convalescent homes, places where people are doing free clinics to help the poor, and other similar social service centers. Now, we have a critical mass where we could gather together as a large group for worship. Also as a regional power, we can think globally as to how those of us from Orange County affect the world devastated by AIDS.

**As a community of believers expands, what methods of accountability do you need to have in place to ensure that finances and power are not abused?**

*Spencer Burke:* Again with the tools changing the rules, I don't see this centralized by any stretch of the imagination. When people can hide behind the institution, it's much harder for people to sniff out a charlatan. It's much easier to sniff out those people who shouldn't be pastors in small church settings. I think the possibility for people to hide in institutions is much greater than in a smaller church.

**How do you see the Internet as a means of building community?**

*Spencer Burke:* I think that the tools change the rules. Within the agrarian society, the tool was the large high steeple in the center of town square where people gathered once a week. Here they found out who was sick, who died, who needed a meal. They also got dressed up, as it was a mating ritual. With the advent of the automobile, you could travel to go to church. Their home often wasn't connected to one's Christian community. You lose and gain things when these tools are introduced. The advent of the Internet has changed drastically many of the rules. For example, I'm part of a male accountability group of twelve men that I've never met, but we meet through conference calling.

**Why do you feel we don't need church to connect to God?**

*Spencer Burke:* It's really important that we define terms. I do not believe that we need the institutional church or brand Christianity to find God. I think the institution is dying, and I think the institution is now more vested in keeping itself alive than keeping the mission it was on. Now, I'm not arguing for us to disband church, but that just like everything else, church needs to evolve. For example, the music industry told us that if we didn't buy vinyl, the music would die and that downloading was piracy and evil. But what happened is iTunes is proving that music will live. Likewise, downloading television and movies, direct TV, and YouTube changed the delivery of movies. The movie industry might die, but movies are alive and well.

# CHAPTER 5

# Leading as the Body of Christ

⦿ BRIAN McLAREN (in person)

**When you were a pastor, what did you do to encourage lay involvement at Cedar Ridge?**

*Brian McLaren:* We had a great advantage because about half of our people were not from religious backgrounds. So there wasn't a shared assumption about a clergy-laity distinction. We tried to teach people that church was a community in which everyone participated. And we tried to model a kind of teamwork that was empowering and horizontal rather than vertical. People in more traditional churches often have to unteach a kind of clericalism that puts them in the mode of customers and clergy as service-providers. That sort of thinking can be undermined by teaching the idea of servant leadership that's so strongly in the New Testament (see Ephesians 4). Also, we have to realize there are symbolic things in our church life that reinforce clericalism—vestments, titles, privileges, and that sort of thing. We're going to have to find ways to counteract those symbolic messages of clericalism so the message of every-member-mission-and-ministry can get through. In addition, we need to find the kind of lay leaders who can complement paid staff. But even using a term like lay people—as I just did—plays into the problem here. I hope someday we get to a place where we just talk about disciples and terms like pastor don't have all that clerical baggage.

**How do you see emerging church as a venue that can encourage a more horizontal form of leadership that encourages lay involvement?**

*Brian McLaren:* The medieval church expressed itself in hierarchies, while modern church was expressed in institutions and organizations. Now, we see the emerging church as an expression of faith in a world of networks. This network becomes more like a gravitational field than a machine. It's a web of relationships where power and information are disseminated very broadly. What I think will happen in this emerging church phenomenon is that we'll find a blurring of boundaries so that old hierarchies and institutions are actually part of emerging networks— they're networked in. As a result, everybody has the capacity to learn from, influence, and enrich everybody.

**What do you see as the obstacles that prevent active lay ministries from developing in churches?**

*Brian McLaren:* Part of our problem is in our heads. In all of our minds we have this jumbled, unintegrated mixture of hierarchical, institutional, and network thinking jumping back and forth. What we need is an integration of these three to tap into the strengths of each kind of organization, all within a more holistic understanding of what the church is, who the church is for, and how the church operates. Right now, we have so many churches functioning in a rather mindless drive for numbers or money or fame or whatever, doing a kind of a broadcast model or show, and more and more people are feeling alienated.

## PHYLLIS TICKLE (in person)

**Any suggestions for how to enable greater participation of the laity?**

*Phyllis Tickle:* This question also has several parts. The one presently nearest to my heart is that of empowering lay teachers, but the question usually refers to the use of lay readers and Eucharistic ministers. Certainly, laity who wish to function in these roles need to be instructed by a liturgist whenever possible, rather than by the priest with whom they are to serve, especially in communions like the Episcopal, Lutheran, or Roman ones where there is a time-honored liturgy in place. All too often, when the pastor or priest does the instructing, the result is an exercise in how to serve him or her and can produce less a traditional and more an idiosyncratic result. I've seen it happen time and time again.

Let me also say, just as an aside, that one must be aware of motives when a congregation seeks greater lay involvement. Putting laity into highly visible positions as a way of getting the focus off of the priest is like putting up candles and rock music and saying, "Look, we're a contemporary church with a contemporary service." It's a fix, it's a Band-Aid, not an evidence of good health.

Let me add here, that in my own diocese, the Episcopal Diocese of West Tennessee, there's a diocesan liturgist, who comes in, when invited, and trains laity. It's also interesting when a denomination can swap lay servants away from the parish where they are members in order to serve at a different altar. For instance, I'm licensed as a lay minister through Calvary Episcopal Church in Memphis in the Diocese of West Tennessee, and as a lector, but my appointment is to Holy Trinity Community Church.

## ELISE BROWN (in person)

**What do you see your role as the pastor?**

*Elise Brown:* I see myself as being an equipper, a facilitator, an infrastructure provider. I'm behind the scenes and helping to create space for the next generation of leaders. I provide feedback for what's going on and stability.

**How do you create that space where the laity feel like they can take full ownership of the service?**

*Elise Brown:* When we started our attentive worship service Common Ground, we had six ordained ministers or people in seminary sharing the message. What that's done is helped the young adult laity feel empowered that they could do the message too. No one person owns the message, but now we're being pushed a bit further to allow the lay team of young adults provide the message, which we're very open to doing. Now, we will continue to have ordained people in the mix for a variety of reasons but don't have a feeling that only ordained people can be in that role.

**Why do you think Advent Lutheran attracts artists and academics?**

*Elise Brown:* We try to find ways to empower their giftedness here. If they're an academic, they might not want to come here and teach a course. They may want to do something that they don't get a chance to do anywhere else in their lives. The key is to find where people's spiritual giftedness is and to empower them to serve in whatever capacity is the right place for them. Any clergy who feel afraid that the laity might "show them up" by being a better teacher or preacher needs to get therapy to get self-aware and be honest about why they feel that way. That's tragic when gifted laity are kept out of serving by clergy's insecurities.

**How do you find and attract lay leaders?**

*Elise Brown:* We find these people by getting to know who they are. We keep them because we utilize them. I think people stay at churches because they are spiritually fed, and they feel like they are making a meaningful contribution. What I've learned in my ministry is if you're going to develop lay leadership that helps a congregation, then the role of the clergy person takes on a very different form. Your office is the equipment room. The pastor is no less visible, but the pastor is serving in a more equipper capacity than being the cult of personality pastor.

**What do you feel prevents mainline churches from pursuing a more horizontal form of leadership?**

*Elise Brown:* I think it's hard for mainline churches to do something that's different from what they've traditionally done. A lot of mainline people like myself can do Lutheran liturgy with our eyes closed. We know all the liturgies by heart. To venture into a new sphere like this not only takes a lot of time, but I think a lot of clergy are so invested in the traditional ways of doing church that they don't think in this emergent way. We have no idea what God is doing for the next generation of people we're called to reach. But I know that right now the emergent movement is drawing young people into the family of faith. Thirty years ago, it was the Chicago folk mass. Twenty years ago it was Hosanna and Maranatha music. Taize seems to have more lasting influence in some communities. Our call is to see where people are in the culture in which we find ourselves and to do as Luther did, which is to try to open up liturgy to the work of the people, opening up spheres of power so that other people can join in and be part of this community of faith.

**What do you say to those church plants who seem to be focused on increasing their numbers?**

*Elise Brown:* Numbers matter in the sense that there's a certain energy and spirit that comes from having people come together. When you see no one coming to an event, it generally means that this is not a space where people are being fed. There's a lot of value in the multiplication model where once a group hits fifty, you need to splinter off so everyone can maintain a sense of community.

✉ MATT, thirty years old, lifelong Lutheran, actor (e-mail)

**What attracted you to wanting to get involved with Common Ground?**

*Matt:* Pastor Brown approached me about it, and I was excited about getting involved with the planning of a new service. The idea of outreach was an important one and something I didn't think I was very good at, so being a part of it would stretch me and my spiritual growth along with all those we were attempting to reach out to.

**What keeps you coming back?**

*Matt:* The fact that it ISN'T a regular service and that anything can, and does, happen. You get to interact more with everyone and have a spiritual experience WITH those around you as opposed to NEAR those around you like in a regular Sunday service.

**What does Common Ground offer that you don't get from a typical service?**

*Matt:* Peace and quiet. I am not getting up and down and having to fit into a "box" when I worship. There isn't an agenda of things to check off (opening, Kyrie, Scripture readings, now sermon, then offering, next is communion, etc.). I feel I can be more myself in God's presence. It's more casual and therefore I am more comfortable and vulnerable; and thus more open to the power of God's Spirit to work in me and through me.

**What are your hopes for this service moving forward?**

*Matt:* I would love to see this service grow in that every service is different from the next in almost every way. I would love to see the message delivered by two or three people and none of them are ordained ministers. There is so much that "everyday" people can offer in leading this service. That is why it's so exciting! With people leading and planning the service who are not "educated" in the ways of church or are bound to what they have been drilled with is the "right way" to run a service, it opens up a whole world of new ways to bring the message to everyone! The possibilities are endless and not contained in a book written by white guys 1,500 years ago. Christianity must change and adapt, and I think the most important way is in HOW the message is delivered. It is the institution of church that scares my generation away. We need to show them what a wonderful community it is and that it isn't going to judge them and their lifestyle but help them to become better, stronger citizens of the world.

## CHERYL LAWRIE:
An Alternative Voice from Down Under

☎ CHERYL LAWRIE (via phone—Skype)

The Alternative Worship Project curates alternative worship and sacred spaces for people who are alienated from the church, or who have never been part of the church. Many of the people involved are searching for a way to be transformed to live differently in the world. They often aren't sure about Christianity—at least the 'version' of it they've been shown.

The project is funded by the Uniting Church in Australia. The UCA has always had creative worship. It could be described as a fairly intellectual church and edges towards the theologically liberal, with a strong public commitment to social justice. The church has always emphasized lay involvement—I'm not ordained.

The project has been going for two and a half years though I've worked for the Uniting Church for close to twenty years. I was a youth worker when I left school and studied theology alongside that. In the position prior to this one I was working on a regional level in leadership development, resource production and congregational change. It was then that I realized that nothing I was doing was making a long term difference. So I quit my job and in an ensuing conversation over a drink with my manager, he asked, "what would you most like to do?" I said that I was going to find a 9 to 5 job, and give my out-of-work energy to alternative worship. He said, "we'll find a way to pay you to do it full time."

And they did. So in some ways the project was a spur of the moment creation. In other ways, it was a deliberate decision by the church to do something that was not trying to change the old but create the new alongside it—to see whether there was another way to make change happen. We started the project with no position description, no project outline, and no anticipated outcomes. We had a hunch that any answers we already had about the change the church needed to make were wrong.

The church has this pattern of behavior where if we aren't sure about a new idea we'll talk about it until the time for the idea has passed. We'll create a committee or task group to research it, and by the time the report is finalized, the moment for that wonderful thing has passed.

We knew we had to bypass that process. We scraped together funding for the project from various bequests and other sources. We didn't go through traditional funding channels, or ask permission for the proj-

**91**

ect, because we just wouldn't have got it. We're now able to access accessing mainstream funding because we now have the credibility. From its beginning the project has been blessed with fantastic advocates—people of power within the church, who fought the battles for me in the church so I was free to do my own work.

From the beginning we realized that the project needed to work outside the existing church—that I couldn't end up doing workshops on worship for congregations. The church can be a very demanding voice! We knew we had to make space to listen to those who haven't had a voice in worship before.

Being involved in this project is such a gift. Accountability to a denomination has been important. It makes me pause and think a little bit deeper. It can also frustrate the hell out of me. But the Uniting Church has created a very generous space that gives us both the support and the freedom to take enormous risks.

I think the alt worship I had in mind was grungy, inner city worship—and that's been a part of it. But the major part of the project has ended up being completely unexpected—curating sacred spaces for people with mental illnesses, for example; curating alternative worship in prisons, working with a little rural house church, designing memorial services for a community of asylum seekers, etc.

My study for my Masters Degree a few years ago has been invaluable to my work with this project. I studied how organizations learn and change and the role of intuitive knowledge within that process. I discovered that the people who lead and go places and effect change are those who know how to learn. They are aware of what they don't know and they keep looking for ways to push their knowledge further all the time. That goes against the conventional wisdom which says that leaders need to know everything before they can lead, but it's especially true when the world is changing rapidly. I think I have to have the same approach to our faith—everything I know is not enough, much of what I know is wrong. I think that's the only way we're faithful.

Writing for [hold :: this space] has become a helpful way for me to think. I put everything up there—liturgies, art space, ongoing thoughts. It's an honest telling of what it's like to try to do worship differently in a postmodern, postchristian context. Hopefully people come by and get inspired and motivated and challenged to try to do something in their own context. I love it when people take stuff and adapt it so that it works. I much prefer that to people coming by simply to take stuff and use it as is—I love it when people add their own flavour.

We're trying to offer worship that's indigenous to the culture here. I have a hunch the more we try to make worship global, the less likely it is that it will work for anybody. When we design worship with a particular group in mind, it seems to have connections that are far broader. When I design sacred spaces, for example, I'll often have one person in mind.

I often feel intimidated when I go to other people's websites and see their successes. But I love that we work out of fragility; to find the resilience that can only be found in fragility. We teeter on the edge of failure because it's at that most vulnerable point that we seem to find something that might connect. We put ourselves out there, find the thin ice and stand over it and see what happens. And sometimes it takes on a life of its own. That's when we stand back and say 'wow. How did that happen?'

At the heart of alt worship is an interplay between culture and theology. Theology has been integral to what we do. I've always thought that the story of the Bible is about the people on the edges finding themselves in the heart of god. Sallie MacFague, in her book *Life Abundant*, speaks of the dangers of theology that is developed from the perspective of white, middle class, male, educated north Americans—theology which assumes that is they are the norm, and everyone else is a deviation (however slight) from that. The Bible speaks to that—it puts 'the other' at the centre. It seems to indicate that we need to look to the homeless, the prisoner, the women, the poor to see the face of God.

I'm wary of parts of the emerging church which are about putting our white, middle class, educated, male theology where 'the other' is. They preach the same message, they just do it in a pub, or at the footy club. What we're trying to do in this project is to discover the unexpected voice of God in this very place—in the prisons, for example, where I'm involved in designing alternative worship, or with asylum seekers. My theology has to get stripped back to its barest bones to have any credibility in these places.

People keep asking if we want alternative worship to become mainstream. I don't think so. Or if it does, I think I'll probably want to keep working on the new thing that's coming behind this. God is always creating the new . . . the test of our generosity will be to let there be space for the new to come up behind us, and to move on past us.

Being on the edge has so much freedom. We don't have to hold everything together. We're allowed to explore, take risks and be radical. We're allowed to not get it right. I worked for so long in the mainstream that I had no idea how much energy I was putting into propping it up.

One of the unexpected things that's evolved has been my writing for the mainstream media. I write regularly for a faith column and some occasional opinion pieces focusing on spirituality for *The Sunday Age*. After each article I'll get emails telling me I'm a heretic, but I also get emails from people saying that the kind of faith I'm talking about resonates with them. A lot of these people have given up on the church but they're looking for a place where their story will resonate with someone else's. I've been surprised by easily people "out there" connect with what we're doing. I think I'd underestimated people.

The web has made so many connections happen. If I hadn't discovered Jonny a few years ago on the web, I wouldn't be doing this. I didn't know you could do this kind of worship. Then, I discovered all these other people through Jonny—Kester, Pete Rollins, Mark Berry. They've taught me so much. I've loved discovering Nadia (The Sarcastic Lutheran). She holds the faith for me. Just knowing others are out there doing what they're doing gives me the confidence I need to push myself into new territories.

I often get asked how to write liturgies. In the same way that most people can't be musicians, not everyone can write liturgy. I think it's important that communities trust that they have the skills they need to create the worship they need to. If you can't write liturgy, borrow it from someone else! Wrap your own music or art around it, and make it yours by doing that. That being said, I only discovered I could write liturgy by practising it over and over. I still throw out a lot more than I use. With alt worship you have to get into a different headspace. Part of my frustration with mainstream worship was that I was often being told what meaning I should get out of the bible passage for the week. What I needed, though, was to be changed by an encounter with this bible story. The starting question in alt worship is 'how can we curate the worship space to tell the story so people can encounter it'? When I write stuff thinking I know what people need to hear it never works. I need to then shift gears, to go back to looking for a way to tell this story. I can feel this shift within my head when I'm working on a space. It comes when I remember that I don't have any answers from God that people need to hear.

I met the guy who does lighting tours for U2. He talked about the process they use to design U2 concerts—they look at a flow of the concert and work out when they want to pull people in and push them back, soothe them and buffet them, and then work out the visuals around that. It's not manipulation. Rather, it's drawing people into a connection between the story of the songs and their own lives. I think alternative worship gives a way to do that with faith.

At the heart of alternative worship is the connection with everyday culture and life. I walk streets of Melbourne for hours and wait for an image to connect to the story. I do my exegesis on a passage but then I try to move beyond the cerebral into an intuitive level. I don't know what encounter people need to hear when they come to church. But I want to create the space so they can hear the story as they need to hear it. It's a highly architected and controlled environment. People seem so much more able to let go when they know someone is in control. We have to make the worship space safe enough for people to take risks.

People in prison teach me about God by pushing my faith into places it hasn't had to go yet—it's also stretched my resourcefulness in planning alternative worship. One of the most challenging things about working in the prison is that it's a prop free environment. I can't take a computer and data projector. I can take in a candle, but no rocks, no fabric, no markers, no newspapers . . . none of the things that I would normally rely on. If I want to use a music CD, I need four weeks lead time to get it approved. Hence, I'm being force to move past every possible alt worship gimmick or short cut and get back to the core.

Added to that, many within the prison community have literacy problems so reading is an issue and they have very low attention spans so talking a lot doesn't work. But we recently did a three week block in the unit for men with intellectual disabilities, writing psalms of lament, anger, hope and boredom. It was moving and profound and incredibly real.

Writing the Easter liturgies for the chaplains to use in prisons was heartbreaking. Good Friday and Holy Saturday were easy—they were days made for prisons!—but how do you tell the story of resurrection within the prison? How do you tell this audacious story of hope without it becoming patronizing, pretentious or arrogant? In the end, the liturgy that emerged was almost a dare to God. We're waiting for this resurrection and it's not happening. Get on with it, God.

Designing worship for within the prisons has kept me honest, I guess. It's meant that I can't get trite. It continually confronts and sharpens my theology. The starting point is what is the story that we need to tell here. I work out of a hermeneutic of suspicion—if the meaning of a story seems to easy for us it's probably wrong. We have to look at it a new way. That keeps me sharp. It's coming back to Sallie McFague—my white, middle class, educated first world reading of the text is probably not the way God meant it to be read.

Sometimes it can ruin it. For example, I ruined Psalm 139 for myself when we wrote up a liturgy for mental illness. I came out with this meditation on how God stalks us like we're on closed circuit TV. I really hate the psalm now . . .

How wonderful it would be to have a few days with people who are doing alternative worship with fringe communities to explore where we might go next. People who are doing this stuff are so few and far between. I really resonate with the stuff Nadia, Jonny, Pete and Mark are doing. There are these points of connection at the fragile moment of what we're doing—but if we tried to formalize something into a moment I think we might lose that spontaneous resonance. Just find the points of resonance and let them live.

To be honest, one of the things that's turned many Australians off from North Americans is it always seems that North Americans come out here with something to teach us and never seem to think they can learn from us. Generosity is two way street—it's about being able to give *and* receive. It's the only way a partnership would work. Similarly, there are some parts of the emerging church in Australia from the evangelical wing that think they have the answers that the church needs but they would have more wisdom to offer if they would hear the wisdom of others, to create a synergy together. I just don't have the energy to keep trying to fit in, to have to explain what we do. The energy involved in that detracts from actually doing what we do!

If we think that we're the next new thing, we're likely to miss out on how God is always creating a whole new thing. We are not finally the church that the world has been waiting for the past 2,000 years. So, we have to focus on how we can be faithful to being the church right here and now. The true test of emergence is how generous we are with the people coming up behind us. Is there some place for them to play, make mistakes and grow behind us.

# CHAPTER 6

# Lift Up Our Voices

✉ JONNY BAKER (e-mail)

**How should people use your book *Alternative Worship*?**

> *Jonny Baker:* Ideally it should be a spark to their own imagination.
> I think it's helpful to get a few ideas and see some of the things other
> people have done. But I always feel we have done something worth-
> while when people tell me about something original they have cre-
> ated or how they have adapted something for their own setting. Then
> it's truly their worship.

**How do you keep the service relevant and real when using popular
music so it doesn't become a concert where the person becomes an
observer instead of a participant?**

> *Jonny Baker:* We don't use music as performance. It tends to be more
> as a soundscape that creates an environment. So, I think this is less
> of an issue for us than for a church with a worship band say. One of
> our core values in Grace, the community I am involved in, is partici-
> pation so to be part of Grace it's difficult not to participate. I don't
> worry about the relevant issue. We try and be genuine or authentic—
> worship comes out of who we are so we can relate to it.

**What do you see as the relationship between clergy and musical director in a worship setting?**

*Jonny Baker:* Alternative worship has broken down this sort of construct. We have a team approach. In planning there will be someone who takes the role for a worship gathering in pulling it together. We call them a curator. Their role is to draw together a creative team and facilitate a process to create the worship experience. This will involve a free flow of ideas and a sharing of who can contribute what. In that process it's natural that a whole range of gifts from different people are used. If someone is a theologian or a liturgist or a photographer or a DJ or an ideas person or whatever, they just offer their gifts to the group and they'll be used as seems appropriate. In Grace we don't employ any professionals—this helps resist the notion of someone being the expert.

**How do you employ technology and visual images into your services?**

*Jonny Baker:* Technology is a tool, so we use whatever seems to fit or is at hand. Our community is pretty web and computer savvy so it's natural to use those tools. But it's not high budget stuff. I think it's a mistake to think if you invest in or get slick technology, it is the answer. Imagination and creativity are what is needed to connect with the culture of the people coming and grow worship from out of the community.

We use a lot of images—again this is natural because we are in a very visual culture—this might be slides, photography, animation, moving images, art, etc. The environment we worship in is important. And it's helpful if it is possible to engage with a number of senses and textures in worship.

**Why should people attend Greenbelt UK?**

*Jonny Baker:* It's a wonderful festival that blends a love for the arts, spirituality, Christ, justice, and the world church. It's very creative. It's a kind of spiritual home for many people who struggle to relate to the church in other places. If you are interested in alternative worship it's a great place to visit, as there are a lot of groups doing stuff in one location.

## ● ISAAC EVERETT (in person)

### What do you see as the relationship between clergy and musical director in a worship setting?

*Isaac Everett:* Well, I've worked with a lot of clergy, and the most common pitfall is the tendency to completely separate the two roles from each other, giving the pastor exclusive authority on theological and liturgical matters while leaving the music entirely in the musician's hands. Not only does this imply that musicians can't have liturgical insights (which is insulting), it also leaves the musician to do the job alone (which can be lonely).

Sometimes, clergy take the opposite tack and want total control, choosing the music without consulting the musician. This type of pastor often picks hymns solely for their lyrical content rather than for their musical qualities. The ideal preacher neither takes control nor leaves a musician alone; instead, he or she makes the musician part of the worship planning process and is willing to engage in mutual suggestion and critique.

To step back for a moment, I personally believe that this whole clergy/musician dichotomy is problematic. It's not something I'm very interested in pursuing myself. Rather than having a dedicated priest and musician, I want to see the whole congregation made into priests and musicians. Martin Luther talked about the "priesthood of all believers" and the broad, folky appeal of his hymns suggest that he believed in the "musicianhood of all believers" as well. The job of professional ministers and musicians should not be to direct liturgical and musical activity, but rather to facilitate them. A liturgical leader's job is not merely to pray and to worship, but to get the entire congregation praying and worshiping. Similarly, my job is not just to play well, but also to get everyone in the room participating in the music; my job is to help everyone find an entry point into the ritual activity.

Also, a lot musicians and performers like to be the center of attention. There's nothing wrong with that—it's probably why we became performers in the first place! Being the center of attention, however, can be a hindrance in facilitating worship, and this is why I think it's really important that every church musician also have a secular career. When I play at a club or in a show, I get to show off my chops, get applause, and hog the spotlight. Once I've gotten that out of my system on Saturday night, I can go into church on Sunday morning and happily step into the role of a worship facilitator.

Having a career in secular music is also useful because it keeps your musical sensibilities fresh. Contemporary Christian music is very 1970s– it comes out of the Vietnam protest era. It's heavy on acoustic guitar and Simon and Garfunkel-ish harmonies. It's not bad music, but it's not contemporary anymore. If you also work as a session musician, however, you get exposed to lots of different stuff and your musical vocabulary stays fresh and current. If every church musician did this, Christian music would really benefit.

**How can secular music become sacred when used in a liturgical setting?**

*Isaac Everett:* First of all, I think this duality is a little bit artificial; any music that's performed in church is sacred music. It's all about context–hearing the same pop song at a concert, in your car, and at church are three very different experiences. I like to use pop music in worship because folks love singing music they know, and they'll be more likely to participate in the music if the music if familiar.

There are lots of ways to incorporate pop music into a service. Even if you don't want to use an entire song, you can take a chorus that everyone knows and use it as a congregational response. For example, many churches pick a verse of a psalm and use it for an antiphon, often in some variety of plainsong, but I like to think of a pop song that resonates with the central message of the psalm and use that as an antiphon instead. I've used everything from the Beatles to Bob Marley to Cake to Damien Rice this way.

**Explain how you made the choices you did for the music on your first CD, *Rotation*.**

*Isaac Everett:* Believe it or not, I'm very passionate about tradition. It's a common misconception that being innovative means that throwing out everything from the past, but there's a lot of room for imagination within tradition. On *Rotation*, I took old hymns, liturgical melodies, and plainsongs and recast them in acid jazz, glitch electronica, and pop. I wanted to show that tradition can be fresh and playful while still being ancient and powerful. Although I got a very positive reaction to my music when I played at General Convention in 2006, some people didn't like it. That's fine. My music speaks to me and my community. Other communities will have different forms of musical expression. The more diversity we have within our tradition, the stronger our tradition will be.

*"The worship this morning [General Convention 2006]
was absolutely wonderful. The music, much of it written
by Isaac Everett . . . was exceedingly powerful."*

—Presiding Bishop Katharine Jefferts Schori

### How do you use visual images in your services?

*Isaac Everett:* I would like to use visuals, but I'm leery of screens and projectors. Having a congregation sit and passively watch a screen is no better than having them sit and passively listen to a preacher. Although a skilled VJ can make ambient visuals, seamlessly blending the images into a larger, multisensory experience, it's also easy for images to be distracting.

For me, the best visuals are real elements in the room with which people can interact. Once, for an Advent service at Transmission, we had a collage station—we set out copies of *Business Week, Glamor*, and *National Geographic* and asked people to find Christ incarnate in our culture. That activity took a lot less effort than preparing a slide show, and it was much, much more effective. It invited everyone to participate creatively, invited everyone to express their spirituality, and allowed everyone present to explore each other's thoughts.

### What did you learn from your first paid gig running an alternate worship service at St. Paul's Chapel in the summer of 2001?

*Isaac Everett:* I was only eighteen when I took that gig. The blogs, connections, and other resources weren't as readily available in 2001, so we ended up trying to invent alternative worship from scratch. We worked very hard to think outside the box, and we did some great stuff, but I don't think we realized how far outside the box it was possible to go.

Trinity Church, Wall Street was very supportive and threw a lot of money at us, but in some ways that hurt us. I'd be in the front of the audience (and I use that word intentionally) playing piano with the other musicians. I'd have a headset on listening to a stage manager in the back who gave cues and coordinated the band with the professional sound crew. The whole thing was scripted and produced like a live television show. We'd get about two hundred people in the congregation, mostly Episcopal clergy from other congregations. It was very sincere, very hierarchical, and very expensive.

Compare this to my experience leading worship at Transmission, where I'm usually sitting on a couch in a candlelit living room with my laptop plugged straight into a home stereo system. During the service, I'll be mixing ambient music live, occasionally bringing in whispers of liturgical tunes. We'll only have ten or fifteen people in the room and none of them are wearing collars. Depending on the service, some people will be praying, others might be doing Yoga, some lighting candles at an icon, and some drawing on mirrors with dry-erase markers. Instead of a stage manager and a priest, everyone helps manage his or her own worship experience, organically encountering each other and whatever activities and themes we have that week. It costs us nothing except the cost of food.

One thing I've learned is that while people like good music, it isn't enough to get them interested in church. It's humbling to realize that music, the thing I'm best at, isn't what creates community. It isn't what people are hungry for. The Episcopal Church often buys into a mythology of "if we make our worship services good enough, people will come of their own accord," but that's just not realistic. Relationships, community, and mission are what bring people into church.

Building a strong community needs to come from the ground up. Don't gather a committee of church professionals and try to target a demographic, instead gather a group of interested people and say, "Let's make church that works for us." As the community grows stronger and stronger, other will people will join it. Organic, community-focused worship will be much more sincere, much more vital, and much more attractive.

I see this kind of misunderstanding in youth ministry all the time. It's really common for a bunch of adults to put on a service they think will appeal to youth rather than putting the service in the hands of the youth and letting them create it for themselves. It's scary to give up so much control, and the end result probably won't be nearly as polished or as theologically articulate as the adults would like, but I guarantee that the youth will be much more invested and engaged in what they're doing.

I've been working on music for a cooking/nutrition show on PBS recently and one of the studies we read demonstrated that children are much more likely to eat food that they helped cook than food that is just placed in front of them. This is just as true in church, and not just for youth. Everyone should be encouraged to actively and creatively engage in the worship-making process.

☎ MARILYN HASKEL (phone)

**What do you see as the relationship between clergy and musical director in a worship setting?**

*Marilyn Haskel:* I would say that in an ideal situation it works best when both people can sit down and do planning together. They can respect each other in terms of what their gifts are and negotiate when there are differences of opinion. In most of the churches I've worked personally I've been allowed to choose the hymns for Sunday. I know there are churches where everybody works in their own territory. I find it works better if it's a collaborative effort. Unless clergy have a specific interest in liturgy, they don't or can't spend the time to explain what the liturgy is to accomplish and how that is to be worked out.

**How do you do a service at St. Paul's Chapel given it's also a tourist museum?**

*Marilyn Haskel:* I'm unsure how long St. Paul's Chapel will remain a museum. We're trying to focus on what we need to do now. For example, we said people could view the exhibits while the church service is going on. We want to bless what is there and to say this is part of who this community is. One time a choir was singing the "Halleluiah Chorus." A tourist walked up to me and asked if they could sing along. That moment struck people who were listening, as they realized they wanted to be a part of this. I have no idea if this was theological, spiritual, or religious, but I could feel it.

**How do you create a community in this kind of an environment?**

*Marilyn Haskel:* It's a challenge to be able to create a worshiping community with people who have never been there and never will be there again. I find I'm composing a lot of music or rewriting standard hymnody so that it makes sense to people who may or may not go to church or be Episcopalians. Yet, I need to do enough repetition so those who do come there regularly, so they will recognize something as an ongoing experience. The music needs to be connected to what the liturgy is about, as well as being easy enough for people who may not have any musical background to sing. When I have a choir that's coming in, they'll sing as if they're the choir for St. Paul's. I just send them the music ahead of time.

**103**

**How can the congregation become participants instead of spectators in the liturgy?**

*Marilyn Haskel:* To get the congregation involved, it takes more than just the right music. It involves how the congregation is greeted and welcomed and put in touch with each other. If you were inviting people to your home for dinner, they wouldn't just leak in the front door. You'd greet them and introduce them to other people. So, church should be the same way. There needs to be an effort to get people close so they can physically interact with each other. If all that is in my place, then my job as the musical leader is to help people connect with that music. I think of myself as an animator to show enough enthusiasm for the work that's being done so it's infectious to other people. Also, I introduce people to the music before the service. Then they have an idea of what it might sound like. It's all connected to the concept of hospitality.

**What lessons did you learn from St. Paul Chapel's attempts in the spring of 2001 to launch an urban alternative service?**

*Marilyn Haskel:* I wasn't on the staff then, but I know that part of what they learned was not to throw money to build a service but to build community. Not enough people had the vision and were on the same page. We took most of the month of December 2006 to talk about the future vision of St. Paul's Chapel. We held congregational meetings to discuss what we wanted and what we might do. Also, we did some experimental liturgy labs where we did some things that we would like to implement at St. Paul's and then we allowed for discussion and input. Once we start doing something, that doesn't mean it's going to be that way forever. We try it and then evaluate it to see if it works or see if it does not. If people have the attitude that if something makes people uncomfortable don't do that again—maybe you should do this again. One of the things we need to get across is that we feel our way along and change things as need be. It's a constant doing, trying, evaluating cycle.

**How do you define sacred music?**

*Marilyn Haskel:* I've had problems with people who draw lines in the sand and saying this is sacred and this is not. Whatever is done musically has to be the something that in the course of the liturgy either helps the action move forward or makes a statement about something that's going on in the service or restate something that's in Scripture. When people do that sensitively and their lives are based in prayers and a belief system, than that will happen.

**What concerns do you have about the use of secular music in sacred spaces?**

*Marilyn Haskel:* I think Sunday morning ought to be a party. We're coming together for a celebration. The word Eucharist means thanksgiving, and there are many ways to do that. That doesn't mean there aren't times within that celebration when one can be solemn. There are seasons when one would be more reserved, such as Lent. I'm only concerned that secular music, if used, be consistent with the gospel and the baptismal covenant: following apostles' teaching and fellowship, resist evil, repent, proclaim the good news, seek and serve Christ in all people, strive for justice and peace, respect everyone's dignity. Secular music can do that if you pay attention.

**What was your take on Isaac Everett's alternate worship service at the Episcopal Church's 2006 General Convention?**

*Marilyn Haskel:* He's very grounded in much of the ancient world, but he's a child of his age and culture. There's no reason why this can't be a blessing in the church as well. I'm a classically trained musician and I love playing song and chanting and I use that at St. Paul's, but that's not the last word in how people connect to the Holy Spirit.

I work with a guitarist who is grounded in the basic hymnody. He works with Episcopal youth and wants to do what he hears on the radio as well. We have a church that's incredibly diverse. That's one of our strong points. What makes this a worship service is not the style of the music or where it comes from, but the dynamics of a room of people who engage in this dynamic and are being present in the space with the Holy Spirit.

The hardest part for people to recognize is what their own culture is and being able to connect with their own spirituality. People feel church has to be different from their own real world. That's not where I live. Someone from a different culture than New York City should be aware of the difference in how they need to do church. For example, small churches think they need to do what cathedrals do, and they can't as they lack the resources and the same culture, and most people are not going to be edified by that at all.

**How can traditional music remain relevant in today's culture?**

*Marilyn Haskel:* We don't want to throw out the baby with the bathwater. Many Roman Catholic churches thought that Vatican II said you aren't supposed to chant any more or sing Latin. So, they got into guitars and went overboard that way. We all do that, we're human. I'm chairing a committee of the Episcopal Church's Standing Commission on Liturgy and Music. We've been given the job of defining worship and praise music (a world collection). The difficulty we've having to differentiate between the Vineyard kind of music and Episcopal music. Also, some churches don't have the ebb and flow within the church year. They have a different structure and they're going to celebrate differently. Liturgical churches have selected Propers and readings appointed for each Sunday. This keeps us honest so we don't neglect the hard parts of Scripture we'd like to avoid.

☎ PAIGE BLAIR (phone)

**Explain the genesis for the U2 Eucharists.**

*Paige Blair:* We don't claim to be the first U2 service, as churches have been using U2 in their liturgies for about as long as U2 has been singing. The movement that became the U2 Eucharist did start here. We started talking about doing this service in May 2005, and found a liturgy from a church called Church Without Walls in Maryland, and polled parishioners and other clergy about their liturgical and musical ideas. We then developed a PowerPoint presentation so we could use visuals with liturgy. An article about our first service in July 2005 ended up on a U2 blog. People from all around the world started contacting us after they saw the story. Every time there's a new wave of media attention, we get more inquiries. This shows the power of good music, good liturgy, and good intent. There's a lot of interest in the Episcopal Church around the Millennium Development Goals, as we ask the question, "How do we work together with God to change the world?"

**How do you structure the U2 Eucharists so that you are within the confines of the Book of Common Prayer?**

*Paige Blair:* We use liturgy from the Book of Common Prayer and every time there's music, we use U2 music. The service we did at General Convention on June 13, 2006, was a very familiar 1979 BCP liturgy. We found that there's power to this when you stick within the tradition, as it shows how traditional U2's music really is.

**How did you prepare the materials so the service can be used by other congregations?**

> *Paige Blair:* This arose from having to answer a whole bunch of questions, as well as from our own experience and taking this on the road. We compiled the answers into one document. Currently, I'm working on a U2 Eucharist book with the Rev. Michael Kinman, Executive Director of Episcopalians for Global Reconciliation.

**What do you see as the future of the U2 Eucharists?**

> *Paige Blair:* As long as the Millennium Development Goals are the number one priority in the Episcopal Church, there will be a role for the U2 Eucharist. At the 2006 General Convention, Episcopalians for Global Reconciliation found ways where we can agree on common goals. Maybe if we do this together, then we can start to understand, hear, and accept each other better. Very conservative and really liberal folks have done U2 Eucharists.

**What do you say to those who say they prefer services with live music?**

> *Paige Blair:* If they have a praise band to do this, God bless them. About a quarter of the U2 Eucharists are done live. We just don't have the resources. Also, we've found that people are used to hearing Bono sing these songs and are comfortable hearing the songs in that familiar way.

**What was your reaction when the service was parodied on *The Daily Show*?**

> *Paige Blair:* Awesome. When you're panned in *The Daily Show*, you've made it. It was quite flattering in its way. What it said is the Episcopal Church is out doing something to make a difference.

# JAHNEEN OTIS:
## A Worship Leader's Musical Journey

 JAHNEEN OTIS (in person)

**What do you see as the relationship between clergy and musical director in a worship setting?**

*Jahneen Otis:* The closest relationship I've had has been with Cannon Lloyd Casson when he was here at St. Mark's. It was almost a synergistic kind of thing. We really connected and became spiritual mentors to each other. It helped because we had family connections. We were sort of from the same tribe. I was considered a member of St. Mark's, but when I took the job of musical director, there were only about thirteen people here on a Sunday including the priest. Lloyd and I walked the streets of the Lower East Side, sat in Tomkins Square Park. The Three Kings celebration that we do every year with music and puppets was really his creation. The Good Friday Blues came about when Nell Gibson introduced me to Bishop Roskam in the Diocesan Convention in 2007. Everybody that participates in that service is a full-time musician and they come to this service so they can worship God.

When dealing with collaborative relationships, you have to be tuned to your gut. I was being considered for a position once at a cathedral. I was so excited about this opportunity. We made all the deals, but when we got down to talking about theology, I pulled out a copy of *Lift Every Voice and Sing*. The canon said this book was sappy and unnecessary. He didn't use that exact term but that was the sentiment. I realized, I can't work here. If you didn't see the validity that a book like this brings, then we can't talk.

**Elaborate on your musical and spiritual journey.**

*Jahneen Otis:* I had been taking piano lessons. My mother was the director of our church choir. She was not a pushy person, but the worship director of the church suggested that I start accompanying my mother. It grew into a job. In addition, my grandmother attended an Episcopal church, so I went to both churches. Both churches that I grew up in were very big, with over six hundred people attending each day.

When I was at Wellesley, I studied music theory and music therapy. I helped to put together all the special events, including a service with Jesse Jackson and the first baccalaureate service with an African American speaker. Another person who inspired me was Paul Santmire. He was getting his doctorate at Harvard Divinity School, and we did a lot of ecumenical services. I felt like we were on this cutting edge of introducing that to Wellesley.

My secular gigs included playing for Kool and the Gang. We played in arenas with over fifty thousand people. That was my first big gig—they mentored and encouraged me to do positive things in the music world.

I have been around artists/activists who had a responsibility to the community for as long as I can remember. My mother was around people who worked with Dr. King and others. I started working with arts and education with Greg Freelon. I really got excited about working on topical theater at NYU. Then I started working with Safari East in the mid-1980s. We were using music as a tool to reach at-risk kids who have been incarcerated. The next step for them is a real lock-up facility. As I got involved with them, I realized that using rap and spoken word as a bridge to the other musical forms such as jazz was the only thing that worked for these kids.

St. Mark's needed an educational outreach program. So, I thought, what would it be like to take the same system and apply it to the church?

George Finger, one of our associate priests, had a connection with a GED program on Henry Street. We worked on programs for creative expressions and it was amazing. At the culmination of this program, I was going to have a party with chips. Then I said, Why don't we have a service and then a party afterward?

The students came up with poetry and songs that connected. There was some concern that the students were going to wreck the building. Also there were those who thought our poster advertising the service was too street. Back in 2000, we did the first hip-hop service that I think has ever been done in the Episcopal Church. Making Marks was the name of the group the hip-hop services came out of in collaboration with George Finger and Beatboxer/Graphic Artist YAKO. It was really about incorporating spoken word into the Episcopal Church. It worked so well that we did a Pentecost service with breakdancers. We did a hip-hop New Year's service and a hip-hop vigil.

Then Bishop Cathy Roskam told me about Fr. Timothy Holder, a priest in the Bronx who was doing hip-hop services. She was thinking that we should combine our energies. So, I talked to Tim and I went up to one of his meetings. At the same time, she was trying to bring together all the clergy in the diocese who were doing alternative worship services. We all got together for a big meeting. The next day, I took the St. Mark's Choir and a band up to the Bronx and we did a hip-hop service with Kurtis Blow and Cool Clyde.

Now, some of the components of Holy Hip Hop, like their teachings on hell and homosexuality, I don't find healing. It's too much fire and brimstone for me. But other than that, I am very supportive of this movement. We need to validate people's lives throughout the week and not just on Sundays. God works through people using music all the time. The North Carolina group "Little Brother" is my pick from the Holy Hip Hop ministries.

I'm a cancer survivor—Hodgkin's. I was on my deathbed. So whatever I've done with my life in the church, it's given me personal peace. If I can't find some spiritual validity in just about everything that I'm doing, then it doesn't bring about the fullness and peace that I need to survive.

**Any words of advice or cautionary tales for anyone looking to launch a similar musical outreach program?**

*Jahneen Otis:* (Laughs) My whole thing with the church was giving back. Because of all the things that were swarming around me, I realize I need to maintain a balance between being creative and giving and knowing what the heck it is you're doing, even though it's an organic process. Some people do that very well. Elizabeth Swados has been an inspiration for me. She's worked on Broadway, and we worked together a few years ago. She's a very organic person, but she's worked with a lawyer to find ways to protect the finished product. She gets a chance to celebrate her work as well as acknowledging other people's input without giving up total control.

The specific caveat I would give people is to be conscious of what the creative process is worth. Just be vigilant about it when you need to safeguard your material. For example, we don't copyright the Good Friday Blues because we're using existing material. I just got a request to share the outline of this service, which I am happy to do. But it's on file and now I do that with all my stuff. The Three Kings Celebration is copyrighted because I work very closely with Lois Bohevesky, and we had come up with specific music and lyrics. But the hip-hop thing was okay, we're putting this on the altar for people to use.

So, I enjoy passing on things, but I do realize that you've got to protect it but do so in a way that you aren't being so overprotective that it kills the creative process. Document your own story. And pay attention to that little voice in your stomach when it tells you something isn't right, so you know to leave. Not every situation is healthy and life-giving and can be salvaged.

Some of our projects like the Three Kings Celebration and the Good Friday Blues get press coverage. I just keep my focus on the work and remember that you're doing this to praise God the creator of this universe and uplift the condition of humanity around you.

Another gift that I have is that I don't have children or a large family. So, I end up being a big sister mentor to a lot of people. With some people like Isaac Everett, I've collaborated with a few times and turned him on to some jobs. When I see people who have that light and divine like D Cross, I help make sure that talented artists like him get an income.

Also, some of us in the music business are accustomed to getting exposure for our work. So we expect that if a ministry takes off and gets a lot of press that everyone will be as generous. That doesn't always happen.

When you're in that kind of an environment with a lot of people around you, you just have to keep yourself focused in prayer and keep your people around you. A lot of this has to do with integrity and your intent. If you stay true to yourself, then you'll be guided where you need to go. You can feel it in your gut when you've stepped too far to the left or the right. If you don't do that, you end up doing yourself in.

# CHAPTER 7

# Transforming Space

 PHYLLIS TICKLE (in person)

> *Phyllis Tickle:* Religion always has an aesthetic to it. There are places that have been hallowed by the prayers of people for many, many generations, places redolent with the religious passion of those who have worshipped there. Yet I am totally sympathetic to the emerging need to get rid of so much of the church architecture that lacks that patina and that so burdens us. Some of those spaces just need something so simple as having the pews that are nailed to their floors ripped up and have portable chairs put in instead to create flexible and responsive space. Sometimes far more is required to turn a space into that which causes the soul to soar. But, nonetheless, you are right that the sense of "classic aesthetic" is not as active in today's applied theology as once it was, or maybe as it should be. I suspect that we could throw out the baby with the bathwater very quickly on this one, too. But many emergent gatherings would, I think, counter what I just said by saying that they are doing creative aesthetics. And I would agree; that is very often true.

 JONNY BAKER (e-mail)

**How do you define Sacred Space?**

> *Jonny Baker:* I am uncomfortable with the language. I think all of life is sacred—i.e., God is present and active in all areas of life and culture.

The church has tended to reduce God's involvement to a spiritual area (church, worship, private morality, and family life). This dualism is pretty unhelpful. So living in London I am interested in how everyday life can be re-infused with God's presence. This is part of the journey of alternative worship—use the stuff of everyday life and culture in church and God's presence will be noticed when those everyday things are encountered in the real world. To give a specific example we used a video of a traffic jam in Lent suggesting it might be a space for solitude and prayer—a desert moment in a busy city. The next time I was stuck in a traffic jam I thought about that idea and used it as such so that space was sacred. Having said all of that I do think it's helpful in the city to have spaces for quiet and renewal. Art galleries can function in that way, as can churches.

**What are some of the more innovative ways you've been able to turn secular places into sacred space for worship?**

*Jonny Baker:* I think the use of the stuff of everyday life and culture in worship enables people to re-imagine everyday life as a site where God is present and active. We have also done several art installation type things that meet spirituality—e.g., Labyrinth, come home, out of nothing, breathe. We have also developed some digital spirituality type things—online labyrinth or iconostasis that make a computer a site for prayer and reflection.

## ☎ PETER ROLLINS (phone)

**Why do you have your services in a bar (or black box)?**

*Peter Rollins:* Whenever Ikon started meeting in a bar, it was a pragmatic decision. I liked this bar and I asked the bartender if I could do it. As time went on, I realized that meeting in a social space was deeply important for us. You hear talk about different types of space, intimate space between a couple, personal space, social space, and public space. Church often feels like intimate space between you and God or private space. So we're exploring inhabiting that social space where all sorts turn up and can be involved. We inhabit a social space and live out our fractured lives in public. We do not take a private room in the back of the bar or meet when it is closed, we just take a regular night and transform it. I don't know many groups who are experimenting with this.

When we're having services in a bar, you get people heckling. It's really scary. But it also created this wonderful dynamic. Some people who could never go near a church find they can go into this bar and explore their faith.

Our most committed regulars are workers at the bar. If we ever have elders at Ikon, they'll be bar staff.

## STEPHANIE SPELLERS (in person)

**How do you create sacred space at The Crossing?**

*Stephanie Spellers:* Our cathedral was founded as the first wholly American church architecture in New England. It's a basic meeting house with box pews and some odd Greek Revival elements. Most people think it's a bank from the outside, and there isn't a lot of classic church "beauty" once you come inside. Given this awkward space, we wondered, What can we do to create life and light in this place, to make it a hospitable place where people feel they're encountering God? So we've collected a closet filled with fabrics we use to bring life and color into an otherwise sensually deadening space. We resurrected some wrought iron pew candles and brought in other lamps, candles, pillows, arm chairs, icons made by folks in the community. Once a week, we use all those elements and do a space transformation. We pull out colors and create levels. We invite people to gather at the holy of holies, to move around in what's otherwise a confining space. We've tried it a lot of ways and we have regular feedback to assess what works and what doesn't. Through experimentation and deep listening, we found there is a live space within this church. It's changed the way everybody sees our cathedral, even on Sunday mornings.

**Your response to those worship leaders who use books like your book** *Radical Welcome* **as a cookbook for how to "make church"?**

*Stephanie Spellers:* Sure, I worry that somebody's going to try to mimic radical welcome the way they saw it in a book, that it'll get gimmicky and they want to copy it. The point is that whatever you do—worship, leadership, ministries, mission—it should be indigenous to the broader culture that you're planted in, and you need to be true to that flow and to the traditions that brought you to this place. I'd encourage those wishing to launch a similar community to explore within their group those spiritual practices and experiences and texts and songs and images and rituals that have opened the way to God for each of them. In church. Out of church. All of it. And then pray and explore together and keep checking in with the wider community to make sure you're not just creating your own little boutiquey, small-group experience. It's about mission. Get out and do it.

**One of the churches in your study was Church of the Apostles (COTA) in Seattle. What could other people learn from watching Karen Ward in action?**

*Stephanie Spellers:* Karen knows how to give other people permission. She has that authority and uses that to open up so that other people can explore the way God has been working in their lives. Also, it's clear in that community that while they are creative, they aren't starting from zero. Rather, they're delving into what is true, authentic, and has meaning in the traditions. It doesn't feel like a typical evangelical emerging gathering. At COTA, they take whatever space they are in and create a place of hospitality that is welcoming to anyone who enters. It's not just how to you turn a tea bar into a sacred space, but how you've made this tea bar a sacred space. You welcome people and see Christ in people in a way they'll never get at a Starbucks.

**Any words of advice for those worship leaders who want to transform a traditional service to attract a younger crowd even though a group of people are being fed by that particular gathering?**

*Stephanie Spellers:* I know that my aesthetics as the pastor aren't the number-one concern. If there's any desire to redesign a gathering, it's got to start with meeting with the people who are getting life from it. Let them say where they've discovered God. Encourage them to push the boundaries, to claim God's movement all over the place and to bring that movement in (or to take the church out) so that culture and church both come to new life. That's how you build the church of the future.

## ISAAC EVERETT (blog)
### Reflections on Space (Spring 2006)

*Isaac Everett:* For those of you who have never met me, I've been making my living as a musician in New York for about seven years now (I like to joke that church-planting is just a really expensive hobby I picked up).

One of the big lessons I've learned as a session musician is that you should never book a gig in a space that's too big for your band. When people are crammed in together, they feel safe. They'll dance, they'll talk, they'll sing along, and you'll have a great gig. When there's a lot of extra room, on the other hand, people feel exposed. They'll be much more inhibited, the energy of the crowd will plummet, and you'll feel like chumps. This is a truism which I've heard echoed by DJs, event promoters, and community organizers. It's also a really important lesson for folks who plan worship.

Example 1: I play for an alternative worship service on the East Side which usually draws about 25 people. We used to meet in the sanctuary, and the service always felt like it was on the verge of dying. A few months ago, however, we started meeting in the side chapel, instead. The service still drew about 25 people, but folks were commenting that attendance had gone up! All of the sudden, people could hear each other singing and started singing in harmony. All of the sudden, it felt like a community and not like a performance.

Example 2: Our two most recent Transmissions had the same number of people in attendance. One ritual was in a member's apartment. Folks laughed, ate lots of food, drank two bottles of wine, and fully engaged the ritual. The last Transmissioner left around 10:30. The other ritual was in the sanctuary of a medium-sized church. Conversations were subdued, no one ate seconds or had wine, and the ritual felt a little forced. The last Transmissioner left around 8:50.

The lesson for church people: There are lots of factors that go into choosing a space (location, facilities, rent), but size is also really important. If you have a hundred people, meet in a sanctuary or an art space. If you have thirty people, meet in chapel or a poetry club. If you have ten people, meet in a living room. If you have four people, meet in the booth of a diner. Don't worry about having room to grow; you can always trade up later.

## Where to Sit in Church

Posted by Isaac Everett on the Transmission blog (www.transmissioning.org), January 23, 2007

*Isaac Everett:* Last Monday, I went up to the Bronx to hear the Presiding Bishop deliver a sermon on Martin Luther King (since I work for a parish in the Bronx, I didn't feel like too much of a carpetbagger). I walked into the service about 15 minutes early but, as you might expect, the place was already filled up. The usher handed me a program and said, "There might still be a few seats in the back corner, behind the choir. Unless you're clergy, of course—we have reserved seating in the front for clergy."

Now I should have said that I was a priest; the New Testament makes it quite clear that there is only one priesthood: the priesthood of Christ. Furthermore, we are all initiated into it by the merit of our baptism, making the entire church a priestly nation.

If I were really on top of things, I could have shouting something like, "Beware of the scribes who like to walk around in long robes and love the best seats in the synagogues! They shall receive the greater damnation!" Maybe I could have waved my arms around a bit to increase the effect . . .

Unfortunately, I'm not that quick on my feet or nearly that snarky. Instead I just shot my girlfriend a look and went to find a seat in the corner. Later on, I remembered that Jesus suggested that we "go and sit in the lowest place, so that when he who invited you comes, he may tell you, 'Friend, move up higher.' Then you will be honored in the presence of all who sit at the table with you." Maybe this is why so many churchgoers like to sit in the back . . .

Anyway, this weekend I had the singular pleasure of helping a bunch of high schoolers plan a worship service for the Cathedral of Western Michigan. These guys did not have reserved seating for clergy. In fact, there was barely any sitting involved at all. The congregation wandered around, did the "Thriller" dance, gathered around the altar in a clump, and threw juice boxes at each other. It might not have been the most nuanced and evocative liturgy I've ever seen, but there certainly weren't any power dynamics on display. It was really, really cool to see how engaged the kids were in making a service for themselves.

And I guess this is why I've found my way into the emerging church. I'm just not interested in seeing worship created for me by an ecclesiastical elite; I want to make worship for myself. I'm not interested in feeling like a spectator, I want to be engaged. I'd rather have my worship feel a little rough around the edges than feel like I'm a second-class citizen.

## ✉ PATRICIA HENDRICKS (e-mail)

*Pat Hendricks:* Sacred space is an atmosphere where people can encounter the presence of God. Today's children, teens, and young adults are experience-oriented. They need to know of God's loving presence both at church and in everyday activities. Various images help set this atmosphere such as pictures, candles, rocks, shells, plants, and Bible stories that are portrayed in art or drama. Participation adds to the atmosphere. Young people like to have a role in the life of the church through preaching, leading prayer, drama, and song.

Ritual is an excellent tool in the creation of sacred space. There is something mysterious about processions, candles, prayers, silence, and communion; and this generation of young people is open to mystery.

Today's young people are involved in numerous activities. Most busy themselves with school, work, extra-curricular events, and a social life. They are tempted by the trappings of popular culture. They are in constant communication via today's technology, and rarely do they experience quiet. Ritual appeals to youth because it provides balance to their busy lives. Ritual invites a person to slow down, to be quiet, and to look to the mystery. Ritual is steeped in tradition that provides a solid anchor for youth.

**119**

Some churches are returning to the use of ritual in its services. Those I interviewed for my book indicated that the shift to incorporating ritual into their services was generally unplanned and came out of the desire of a few people. In one case, a group of young adults began an alternate Sunday service based on a simple ritual of short Scripture reading, conversation, silence, and prayer. In another instance, a courageous youth pastor slowly began to introduce images and softer music into her worship services. Some young people told me they used the "trial and error" method. They tried some ideas and paid attention to the response. Others spent time in prayer with the core group to discern how to create ritual.

Worship leaders of the emergent churches I visited chose images to help people focus on the presence of God and the theme of the service. Those images often included objects of nature, photographs, Christian symbols, colorful fabric, candles, and softer music. Those images were chosen by a core group of people who prayed and discerned the focus of the evening. From this, I can conclude that the emergent service is community driven rather than program driven. It is not based on what other churches do; nor is it based on a "canned program." The service emerges out of the hearts and prayer of a core group.

I did notice that, other than the use of PowerPoint to display photographs, there was very little technology used. I can only speculate that people who attend emergent services are saturated by technology and are drawn to services that are simple and are real rather than virtual.

# CHAPTER 8

# Melding Ancient Spiritual Practices with the Modern Culture

☎ KURT NEILSON (phone)

**Define ritual, and how do you see ritual as being redefined for the twenty-first century?**

> *Kurt Neilson:* I am not sure there is a need to "redefine ritual." The need for ritual, to structure and experience safely the key transitions of life using ancient symbols and stories and in the context of a larger community, is a human constant. I have been moved by efforts by Seattle's Church of the Apostles (COTA) and others to make traditional wisdom like the spirituality of icons, chant using PowerPoint, light imagery using traditional taper candles, available and accessible to a new generation, or disaffected members of the present generation (the "dechurched"). At Saints Peter and Paul, we are low-tech and conventional—chant and incense the "old way," pipe organ, no screens. But we are open to new formats offered at other-than-Sunday-morning times.
>
> People hunger for Christ, for Trinitarian life and community. Identify that people want prayer and regular discipline and community, and be open to new ways in which to experience this—Office prayed using web resources, blogs, whatever it takes to find new ways to practice ancient faith.

**Which populations do you feel are especially drawn to these ancient spiritual practices, and why?**

*Kurt Neilson:* Younger-than-Baby-Boomer folks: members of my own generation are still mired often in "rebelling against the Establishment" and deconstructing beyond meaning every traditional image or resource. What Boomers don't get is that such zeal is not a universal—it is culturally conditioned and has hit its expiration date. Younger folk don't have any interest in gathering and hearing why they no longer have to believe the story-as-it-was-told-when-they-were-little. There is no more "establishment" as envisioned by the "Me Generation." All there is left is an economy, and a crushing array of people and forces willing and eager to sell everything to blocks of people identified as a "demographic." Churches of all ilk fall into this same anxious, predatory pattern of selling, and many denominations have unapologetically adopted wholesale marketing techniques and called it "evangelism." Younger folk do not want Jesus sold to them as a commodity. They want a faith that is free and authentic and are open to manifestations of that faith that have stood the test of time and might throw a little light on an alienated and market-driven age.

**Some would say that an Anglo-Catholic Episcopal Church with an open progressive theological outlook is an oxymoron. Your response?**

*Kurt Neilson:* According to some homegrown manifestations of "Anglo-Catholic," it may be. I have found that for some, "Anglo-Catholic" is a brand name for everything they are against: women in leadership, the twenty-eight-year-old "new prayer book," and to that is added whatever has offended or upset the individual complainant. The intellectual breadth and generous latitude of Anglicanism can often permit such a subjectivity that allows the disgruntled individual to ignore the whole sweep of Anglican, Catholic, and Reformed history. But I would answer that the reappropriation of the conversation with the depth and riches of the Catholic heritage in the Anglo-Catholic revival is at its best when it uses such tradition, the "living faith of dead people" as said Jaroslav Pelikan, to equip us to live a passionate Christian life that is at the same time open to the hard questions posed by the unfolding of the world's history and the real lives of those surrounding us. This does not mean that we will be in complete agreement, nor should we be perhaps. But it does mean that we will hold essentials in common and acknowledge one another's differences in love and charity, and not engage in the kind of disdain and exclusion that makes us such a laughable spectacle to a postmodern and "post-Christian" culture. Such games are a man-ifestation of what Pelikan called in turn "traditionalism," the "dead faith of living people."

**How does the Columba Center (named after St. Columba of Iona) ground your church for its work to the homeless and women in prostitution?**

*Kurt Neilson:* The grounding is in the recaptured narrative of a Celtic monastery at its best—nurturing a passionate Catholic/Celtic/monastic spirituality at its center, welcoming pilgrims and reaching out to the broken. Retelling a rich and traditional narrative enkindles a deep spark of acknowledgement in hearers who have been nurtured by word and sacrament, almost a corporate memory of where-we-have-been and can be again: "I remember this!"

## CATHERINE ROSKHAM (in person)

**How do you encourage churches that want to stretch the boundaries of their worship services given the confines of the Book of Common Prayer?**

*Catherine Roskham:* I think it's really important, that if we're going to say that what unites us is our common prayer, then we have to be faithful to the authorized text. I don't think we can have it both ways. One of the things we've said is we allow a wide spectrum of thought because we're not a confessional church. We are not unified in doctrine; we're unified in our worship. So, I tend to be conservative on anything hav-ing to do with the prayer book. It is the glue for the way we understand ourselves to be bound together, and so therefore we need to treat it with tremendous respect. Having said that, I also think there's great flexibil-ity in the prayer book itself and all the options that it allows. In addi-tion, the two volumes of *Enriching Our Worship* offer further alternatives that are also authorized for use. All of these texts allow leeway for dif-ferent practices and the use of alternative or original material in such sections as the Prayers of the People. We have to exercise some caution in using original material because I do believe that *lex orandi, lex cre-dendi.* I think that the way we pray is the way we believe. Sometimes the temptation is to go off on our own and say things that seem great at the time but turn out not to be very good theology. You can always draw from prayer books from within the Anglican Communion for Prayers of the People and Collects, but I also think there is something to having an indigenous book. Our identity as American Episcopalians

**123**

has made a contribution far wider than people are willing to admit to the ethos of our communion. I don't think we should lose that.

Also, being an old theater person let me put it this way. Production values are as important as the script. That "script"—the drama of a Eucharistic liturgy—has had a run of close to two thousand years and is still going strong. We know we have a good drama: It's the paschal mystery unfolding in the Sunday by Sunday celebration of the resurrection. Eucharist is an event; it is an occurrence, Christ becoming present in the midst of God's people. And I think when we read liturgy like we're responding to a grocery list, when we read Scripture like, "Oh we've all heard this before," it become very dull. Every Eucharist, every reading of Scripture is the first time. And it's not just that we need to do Eucharist *as if* it is for the first time, it *is* the first time in a particular gathered company in a particular place and in a particular moment in time. I think that if that's our stating point, then we're already ahead of the game. We can do liturgy it in a variety of styles. I think variation of music can certainly set a tone. Cultural context is important as well. The Latino community has brought wonderful music and a wonderful style to the North American church. So we can honor all that and still be true to our understanding of ourselves.

### What role can bishops play in helping to encourage and grow such ministries?

*Catherine Roskham:* I think that in our polity if a bishop doesn't want something to be done, it's not going to happen. Conversely, bishops can make things happen by helping to cast a vision and set a tone that encourages this sort of development. In my opinion, every bishop is a missionary bishop. Therefore, it behooves us to take different liturgical forms seriously because we're not simply ministering to establishment. We're on a mission and hence, we need to learn a lot of vernaculars, musical, verbal, kinetic, in order to spread the gospel.

### Why are you supportive of Hip Hop within the church?

*Catherine Roskham:* I was in on the writing of the *Hip Hop Prayer Book*, and my rule of thumb was it's got to be translation. It's not a new book, it's a new translation. Now, I know it offends some people but those are not the people for whom we did the prayer book. We're not trying to inflict this on people who don't like it. And we don't expect that our churches will be doing Hip Hop Eucharists at 11 o'clock on Sunday morning. It's a gateway for people into our tradition, which can at times seem a bit obscure to folks who are not from a Northern European Anglo tradition. We do it for those people for whom hip-hop has meaning and resonance so that they might come to know Christ. That is certainly part of our tradition.

**Why do you participate in St. Mark's Church-in-the-Bowery's Good Friday Blues and their Three Kings celebrations?**

*Catherine Roskham:* I had been involved with St. Mark's-in-the-Bowery principally because of Jahneen Otis. She is not simply a musician, but she's really a music minister. And we began doing the Good Friday Blues some years ago. We dramatize St. John's Gospel. We do not change it, but we go further in dramatizing than most churches do, say, on Passion Sunday when parts are given out to be read. We punctuate the action with short homilies and music from the blues tradition and from spirituals. Both of those traditions have their roots in the crucifixion experience of slavery, so they seem particularly appropriate for use on Good Friday. It's deepened the Good Friday experience for those of us who have taken part in that liturgy every year. It's Bible and it's prayer book—but in a different style.

**When do you know when a cutting-edge ministry requires your intervention, and how do you handle these situations?**

*Catherine Roskham:* There is such a thing as the doctrine and discipline of the Episcopal Church, and bishops do have the say over the liturgy of their diocese. So, certainly you can depend on the canons for a bishop's ability to come in at any point and say, you can't do this. But I don't think that's the model. The model is partnership where the parameters are explored as these liturgies develop, so there are no last-minute surprises.

**So if someone was trying to do something innovative within the Episcopal Church, their first step should be to contact the bishop?**

*Catherine Roskham:* Well the bishop should be notified of any liturgical changes. I believe that's in the canons. I think that when you're not talking about Sunday liturgy, you have a lot more leeway. And I think most bishops feel that way, too.

**Any resources you've found to be helpful?**

*Catherine Roskham:* I don't use books for this work; I use people as a resource. This kind of work is very contextual, so you can't always get it out of a book or a program resource. So we're very lucky in the Diocese of New York. We're in the middle of a place where musicians and actors and other kinds of talented folk come together, so we can draw this wonderful human resource to help us stretch our artistic boundaries.

## PETER ROLLINS (in person)

**Define ritual, and how you see ritual as being redefined for the twenty-first century?**

*Peter Rollins:* The ritual is of central importance to what we do at Ikon. It's the place where we symbolically interact with the ideas being explored in the gathering. In the ritual we try to maximize the use of all our senses by thinking of actions that communicate at a different level than words.

We have also delved deeply into the Orthodox, Catholic, and Anglican traditions in an attempt to learn what rituals have been used in the past and what their purpose is. We attempt to remain faithful to these rituals by reimagining them in a different context. While we may be sitting in a dingy pub reading liturgies scrawled on the back of beer mats rather than chanting Latin in a basilica, there is often more similarities than you would first imagine.

**How do Ikon's services put into practice your belief that the truth in Christianity is not described but experiential?**

*Peter Rollins:* In a sense I would not even want to say that the truth of Christianity is experiential in so much as the truth of Christianity is life, and life is not experienced. Rather life is what allows us to experience. Just as one does not see sight, but it is sight that enables one to see. In other words I don't think we experience the truth of Christianity, but the truth of Christianity is hinted at in the renewed way we experience everything else. In this way the truth of faith is not one thing among other things but rather is that which brings us into new relationship with all things.

The way we explore this within Ikon is by attempting to create a gathering in which Christianity is not fundamentally about an understanding or experience but rather a way of being and interacting in the world.

**What do you say to people who want to mimic what you do at Ikon?**

*Peter Rollins:* It is a great honor when people want to take stuff that we have done and repeat it. However we want to encourage people to take the bits they like and create something new. We don't want to limit creativity but rather to encourage it. Ikon is not the kind of thing that can be packaged whole and sent around the world. Although I do believe that underling ideas are not limited to a regional location.

**Why do you say that Ikon is like a safety label on medicine?**

*Peter Rollins:* Well take the medicine as a church, then Ikon can be seen as the label that says something like "This medicine is good for you, but if you take too much it could cause drowsiness, have laxative effects and become addictive." In short, we try to remember that the churches we are a part of are as dangerous as they are important and can be a block to God just as they can provide a way of access to God.

**What do you say to those for whom Ikon is their only "church" experience?**

*Peter Rollins:* For me, Ikon is not set up to be an alternative to church, although for some it is. For most people Ikon is simply one small part of their life. We do not attempt to be like Wal-mart—we don't have all your goods under one roof. We are more like a village shop, important to the village but not the most important thing. People who look to explore faith only with Ikon will end up missing all the other wonderful stuff in the village. Most people who attend do not then take Ikon as their only religious outworking because it does not provide enough on its own.

## ✉ NADIA BOLZ-WEBER (e-mail)

**How does the Lutheran liturgy inform your work?**

*Nadia Bolz-Weber:* Our liturgy, which is this gift handed down to us from generations of the faithful and which contains a wisdom to be cherished and to not be dispensed with, but allowed to wash over us in worship and to pattern our lives. By immersing ourselves in this mystery narrative through the weekly Eucharist and the seasons of the church year, we walk through the world with dual citizenship in the now and the not yet. It would take a great deal of hubris on my part to think that I can "come up with something just as good." Having said that, I think we've only begun to see the creative possibility and potential cultural expression of the liturgy. That's exciting to me, but to innovate with integrity I am convinced that one must be deeply rooted in tradition.

## How do you work within the confines of your synod?

*Nadia Bolz-Weber:* I am currently in the candidacy process for ordination in the ELCA. I respect the Lutheran Church and feel that there is not enough wrong with it to leave, and there is just enough wrong with it to stay. My synod and the ELCA are faithfully trying (as much as an enormous bureaucracy can) to see what God is up to in the world and to try and join in. They are allowing me to do an emerging church plant as my internship, which is unheard of.

## What is your role as pastor for the theology pub?

*Nadia Bolz-Weber:* I prefer hostess to pastor. I created the theology pub so that there was a space for people to have an open theological conversation. When do folks really get the chance to talk about faith and prayer and God and religion where no one is questioning their orthodoxy or trying to convince them of "the truth"? It's important to me that everything is on the table and that the conversation not be too academic or too "churchy." We get totally unchurched people, ex-Catholics, gay Unitarians, members of AA, seminary students, pastors . . . a whole range of beauty.

## What do you say to those who feel all you have to do is light some candles, turn down the power praise music, and voila—you have an emerging church service?

*Nadia Bolz-Weber:* "You're an idiot." Um . . . I mean it's really hard for a modern church to get away from the idea of "targeting a market." I haven't really heard of it working for a traditional church to hire a guy with a goatee who says "crap" and can light a few candles to then have throngs of postmoderns joining their congregation. This can often be a bit of a theological bait and switch where under a thin veneer of cool is a theology that still sucks.

✉ JONNY BAKER (e-mail)

**How do you define ritual?**

*Jonny Baker:* Ritual is embodied participatory action. I am a big fan of ritual. It can be transformative. Some ritual creates a liminal space—something like the labyrinth does this. The use of the labyrinth enables the walker to take that experience with them back into everyday life.

**What do you say to those people who feel that by lighting some candles and playing ambient music, they're creating emerging church services?**

*Jonny Baker:* It's easy from the outside to focus on style. But the reason for the emerging church is much more about re-imagining what it means to follow Christ in a different (emerging) cultural context. The style is irrelevant. What works in one context will be entirely inappropriate in another. The key is missional imagination.

🧍 ELISE BROWN (in person)

**Why did you decide to start an alternative worship service titled Common Ground?**

*Elise Brown:* We decided that we had an opportunity as a mainline church in the city to venture out into some unknown territory. No other Lutheran churches in the city were doing an alternative kind of service. So, we thought we would take the strength of all the young adults we have and galvanize their energy and their creativity and see what emerges.

**Explain the planning that went into launching Common Ground.**

*Elise Brown:* The planning for this service went on for almost a year and a half before the actual launch. We had a team of about twelve people, who had various gifts that we thought would be helpful. We brought them together and split them into six subteams. The group basically worked very organically to structure the themes and the flow of the services, as well as the way that outreach would be conducted for the services. While most of the people are still on the planning team, some have left and others have come on board.

**129**

**Any advice you'd give to someone looking to launch a similar service?**

*Elise Brown:* Make sure the music is set up and in good order. That's a major piece of making a service like this succeed. Make sure that it's organic, that it's coming from the bottom of the community's gifted-ness rather than some kind of top down approach. Make sure that the group itself owns what's happening. Don't be afraid to take risks and let go of the traditional notions of power base.

Fear of failure keeps people from trying anything. Reach out, try something new, then see where it goes and what happens. See if leaders emerge, and if they don't, that's okay too. We're so afraid of failing that we don't try and that's sad. My first exposure to emergent was at the Festival of Homiletics in 2005. There were a couple of guys from California who did a simple service that was just awesome. It was the best emergent experience I've had yet. Before launching Common Ground, I went to a lot of different services to see who is being reached by this service. I've been to a lot of services where it felt like it wasn't happening. I found some services are still very much paper driven. We didn't want for Common Ground to be another bulletin-led service where everyone had their face in the paper. Also, I found a lot of theology-lite going on out there with a real superficiality. They make it so user friendly that there is no substance there, which does not go well with Lutheranism, which has this deep and profound theology of the cross.

**How do you keep the service grounded?**

*Elise Brown:* There is a natural fear of venturing into the unknown and letting go of what we know. In order to remain relevant in our culture, I think we have to show openness to new forms. I'm pretty confident in our leadership. They're all part of our church in some way. The group is basically grounded in the theology of the Lutheran Church. We've had a few experiences of theological weirdness. But when that happens, we just provide the feedback and trust that people can be open to hearing what we're saying. By and large, it's worked. We've had to make shifts and changes along the way and examine and reexamine things.

**Even though this service was targeted for young adults, how do you see it as having an intergenerational appeal?**

*Elise Brown:* It creates a natural space for people to come together and have some social time. A service like Common Ground is not for those who need an ordered, predictable worship experience. It's more for a creative, free-floating spirit, who aren't threatened by being asked to share with people around them, whom they don't know. We did find that people responded well to things such as the lighting of candles because it's something that's such a part of so many faith traditions, and it's very accessible. I think when people are forced to speak, that's when they get a little bit off.

## How do you see ritual as being redefined for the twenty-first century?

*Elise Brown:* I think we long for rituals in our lives. There are rituals for going to the movies, the theater. We are a human organism who longs for some kind of order. So, at Common Ground, we actually follow a form. We've made to changes to it, but there's a basic skeletal form. We sing some of the same songs like the creed each time, so people become familiar with it. For some people, that provides comfort and they join right in.

## How does Common Ground fit into the overall worship of Advent Lutheran Church given it isn't your traditional Lutheran service?

*Elise Brown:* Most surveys will show that if you start a new service and you have existing services, it will cannibalize off of your services. When we first started Common Ground, there was an overall decrease in Sunday morning attendance. There's an initial dip, but then if you're a growing organism, then the growth occurs. Interestingly now, our Sunday morning attendance has strengthened.

## ☎ KEVIN GOODRICH (phone)

## How does the Anglican tradition inform your work with the emerging church culture?

*Kevin Goodrich:* I've seen a great interest in the emerging generations and the emergent church, specifically in holy tradition—the mystics, monks, the Eucharist. They are interested in these things, but want to apply them squarely in the middle of twenty-first-century environments. As Anglicans we are the middle way between Protestantism and Roman Catholicism. This makes us, I believe, the perfect church to engage the emerging culture's desire both for ancient spirituality and contemporary application.

## How do you work within the confines of the Anglican book of prayer and the church hierarchy?

*Kevin Goodrich:* Ironically, the prayer book, a hallmark of identity for Anglicans has become something of a stumbling block for us. I say ironically because the prayer book was an innovation designed to make the worship life of the church accessible to the public at large. Innovating worship mediums is part of our tradition, but in many cases we've become landlocked with the prayer book as is. We should be asking ourselves how we can make worship accessible to a culture that is no longer textual (as it was becoming when the first prayer book came out), but is now principally visual in orientation. As for the hierarchy, I believe in a God-given leadership structure for the church. However, the key here is flexibility, and in many cases our current diocesan structures for leadership, clerical formation, and canon law work against us. We need to reform and revitalize these for a post-Christian culture and for a church that must be centered on mission and not establishment.

### What are the challenges of talking about emergent church in North Dakota?

*Kevin Goodrich:* While the culture is changing, one of the challenges is the strong vestiges of Christendom. People value the church as an institution that contributes to the social order of society. More so then other parts of the country, people have a strong sense of historic affiliation with a particular Christian denomination (particularly Roman Catholic and Lutheran) even if they lack any active involvement in a local congregation. We have these historic ties, so people think they're operating in a Christian society even though the churches are declining. There is a need for education about the biblical foundations for what the church is called to be versus what it has been in American society at large. In some ways the culture here has to change more before the population will fully wake up to what is happening. This is in contrast to communities I use to serve on the East Coast where the changes were quite evident to all.

### What are other challenges you face, which are unique to the heartland?

*Kevin Goodrich:* One of the big challenges is the decline of community life in small towns. What the broader culture is looking for is here, but it's dying. People long for what it was like twenty to thirty years ago. We don't face an urbanization of culture and geography, but through the media young people see a world that is nothing like their own locally. So, we have problem of keeping young professionals as our population continues to age.

**What can rural churches bring to the dialogue that's fresh and unique?**

*Kevin Goodrich:* Our proximity to nature and the fact we are smaller, so people tend to know each other is an advantage in some ways. We still have a sense of communal life that's been lost in part of the coasts. One of the most prophetic needs is for the church to promote the Sabbath and the need to be unplugged. Here that's easy as you have to drive a long distance to get anywhere and we have all this huge open space. Also, as we don't have a lot of money as a diocese, locally trained priests without benefit packages serve almost all of our churches. So you get a lot of farmer-priests and teacher-priests. The culture of the seminary doesn't always adequately reflect the culture of where people serve. But the priests here already know the mission field; they're natives. You just have to raise them up, and they're ready to go right away.

**Define ritual, and how do you see ritual as being redefined for the twenty-first century?**

*Kevin Goodrich:* I see ritual as being prescribed language and symbol patterns for the encounter of God. That's the meat and drink of our worship services as Anglicans. Modernism is textual based with a focus on words and a rational systematic way of thinking. If you go to the most traditional Anglican services, it's a very sensory experience–people touch books, walk to altar, and kneel on wooden pews. The emergent prayer rooms I've seen are often taking things out of our tradition and using it to create a multisensory worship experience.

☎ RICK FABIAN (phone)

**Explain how the Episcopal Diocese of California created St. Gregory of Nyssa Episcopal Church in 1978.**

*Rick Fabian:* We put together a five-year plan in consultation with the other rector Donald Schell. This was not an alternative ministry but a study of things that had gone on in the past and what we'd like to do in the future. The diocese had the choice to open a new parish and decided to do that.

My guiding principle to anyone building or remodeling a space is to get a good acoustical engineer in at the beginning of the work. Along those lines, the principle we followed at St. Gregory's was that there has never been a good acoustical space that was ugly. The plan for St. Gre-

gory's is on our website (http://www.saintgregorys.org/Pages/PlanSGN
.html). A great deal of scholarship by other people is in the background
of the plan.

### How does your worship and liturgy carry on the teachings of St. Gregory Nyssa?

*Rick Fabian:* His teachings show up pastorally. We don't know anything
about what he thought about liturgy. As we take it for granted that
everybody is on a path to God, we ask people at the sermon time to
stand up and share their experiences. If you look at God, there's nothing to see but darkness but the reflection of God on other people's lives
is what you guide your life by. People making progress toward God is
Gregory's big word.

### How does your liturgy enable you to fulfill your mission "to invite people to see God's image in all humankind, to sing and dance to Jesus' lead and to become God's friends?"

*Rick Fabian:* Everything that we do is based on historical, liturgical, or
social study. We had created a participatory liturgy and went forward
in the direction the prayer book writers had picked out in learning from
tradition to enhance participation.

In every service, we work to make God's conversation with all
humanity show up. For example, over our altar table is a super life-size
icon of saints and animals dancing. That dance represents a teaching of
Gregory of Nyssa—once there was a time when the whole relational creation formed a single dancing chorus looking up to the leader of this
dance, and the harmony of motion that they learned from his law
found its way into their dancing. The saints, who are nominated by the
congregation, come from different cultures. Their lives show progress
toward God usually by crossing some boundary or another. For example, you have Malcolm X dancing with Elizabeth I of England, as well
as ordinary people and animals.

### How can liturgical dance and music be incorporated into a worship setting without it becoming a spectacle where the congregation become spectators and not participants?

*Rick Fabian:* You can see from all the councils throughout the Middle
Ages that tried to stop dancing that everyone was dancing in church.
The custom survived at University of Cambridge until end of eigh-

teenth century. The Shakers and the end of Methodist revivals were holdovers from the past.

Liturgical dancers can get stuck performing on stage because a church hires them to do a performance instead of making it an interactive performance. For people who want to launch dance in the congregation, I'd start it at the midweek service, which tends to attract older women. They love to dance and nobody asks them to do it. We use simple repetitive Greek steps that everyone can do while we sing hymns. Also, we use the dance hymn for more than one week at a time, so everyone feels comfortable.

### Why did you choose to open the Scriptures by singing the Shema?

*Rick Fabian:* The oldest use of the Shema is to open the Scriptures. This act shows continuity between Christian and Jewish worship. We bring out that continuity because we share one worship tradition. Our service also includes Greek elements that are not Jewish at all, such as the Eucharistic banquet that's Hellenistic. We sing the Lord's Prayer with all the physical gestures that developed in monasteries in Syria. Muslims picked up these gestures from Syrians and it's what we see them use today.

### How can traditional music remain relevant in the twenty-first century?

*Rick Fabian:* We have a number of composers at St. Gregory. Writing music for a congregation to join in can be difficult as it's a challenge to write melody. Melody trumps everything as a composer. You've got to come up with melody that everyone will join in with their hearts.

More of the music that Americans encounter is stuff they feel they can participate in is reduced to rhythm with a very little melody, such as rap. Also, most of our melodic singing these days we hear on the radio is solo work and there's less corporate singing in public. Sacred music is not intrinsically different from any other music, but we have few models to pull from in the public. Any style will work provided it has, most important, melody and a way for people to join into it with harmony or rhythm.

The current Episcopal hymnal and prayer book decided to include music that can only be performed with instruments. That's more challenging for people to do because participation means singers have to follow the instruments because of the rhythmic complexity of the songs.

The 1940 hymnal brought into standard use in Episcopal churches of a long tradition of popular singing based on French carols and German chorales. Everything came out in four parts, which was developed in the seventeenth and eighteenth centuries, and it became very popular. That's a tradition that was constantly in touch with folk music. We don't know who wrote it as pieces picked up orally. The modern composer has to decide how to connect with the tradition of participator singing based on folk roots. The challenge today for a composer is that modern academic serious composition music is not designed like that.

Thanks to private publishing and the Internet, you can circulate stuff today in a way that music used to be circulated only orally. Stuff goes around and you can find out in a short time if it's relevant. That's an advantage we didn't have twenty years ago.

**Define ritual, and how do you see ritual as being redefined for the twenty-first century?**

*Rick Fabian:* Ritual is what people consciously and deliberately choose to do again. I think that's a good social and psychological definition. And the question now with ritual is for us, How will we do things in the first place so people say, I want to do this again? Secondly, do they feel this is something we are doing together so that in this ritual, you're together not only with the people in this room but connecting with Christians from other countries and in ancient times? Our church is full of both Christian and non-Christian folk art from all over the world. One of the objects I'm most proud of is a Shinto family shrine of exquisite construction. We're doing this in fellowship with faithful, religious people in Japan who are not Christian. It is possible sometimes at a safe distance to bring together things that are in other circumstances would produce painful memories. This is also true of using Jewish ritual in services. We're very careful to bring out the continuity of things we have in common with Jews and Christians. For instance, when we do a Seder at St. Gregory's, we bring in a rabbi to do her Seder. We don't try to Christianize this.

**Where does tradition fit into this debate?**

*Rick Fabian:* We treat tradition as a storehouse for participation. We don't appropriate the stuff that's nonparticipatory. Things that are there are there because at one time they were popular. You have to be careful to say you can throw stuff out. The musical world is full of rediscovery. Stravinsky rediscovered folkdance. Mendelssohn rediscovered Bach.

Seventeenth-century music is hot right now. But you can't do the music the way they did it during that period. For starters, all the documents say people played the music differently in London versus Paris. What will spur our work is to recover the experience people had in the seventeenth and eighteenth century that everything they heard was new performances. It's like jazz—innovative and experimental, while emphasizing individual reinterpretation.

**Which populations do you feel are especially drawn to the reinterpretation of these ancient spiritual practices, and why?**

*Rick Fabian:* Our average parishioner is about forty, which is young for an Episcopal church. The people who come to us are open and willing to try something that they have not tried before. It's not a surprise that most of the people who join St. Gregory's are in some kind of a life change anyway.

## STEPHANIE SPELLERS (in person)

**How do you work within the confines of the Book of Common Prayer when incorporating the contributions of other traditions into the liturgy?**

*Stephanie Spellers:* There is a basic structure to the gathering (the ordo): there is the gathering, the word, the prayers, the table, the blessing, and the sending forth. Anglicans gather at the table and remember in a profound way that Jesus is right there at that table with us. It's not just a memorial. And we have an incarnational understanding of God's life in creation. So we're able to look around at the culture and the creation and say, hmm, it never occurred to me that God was showing up in that kind of music, or those kind of images or this particular person. But it seems that God is there. To me that's a quintessentially Episcopalian, bonafide Anglican perspective.

I've very grateful to be in a diocese where we have the freedom and permission to explore. We're being told "go." At the cathedral we're using resources from other parts of the Anglican Communion. It's not just at The Crossing. Sunday mornings at St. Paul's Cathedral is probably one of the most radically welcoming experiences I've ever had. We follow the order of the 1979 Prayer Book, but we aren't limited to the rites from that book. You'll hear as much from New Zealand, Ireland, England, and other churches and America, and that makes sense because this is a multicultural church.

I think it's all about authority and whether it's used to control everything or whether it's used to shape something for the sake of a

**137**

higher goal: deeper communion with God and our neighborhood and world. Bishops have the authority to order the worship in their diocese. But Thomas Cranmer and the founders also declared that the rites of the church need not be the same in every place, you have to take into account the exigencies of the time and that things may be different. I think it's important for a bishop to give guidance and permission, to say, "You may need to do things in a slightly different way. You do need to refresh our traditions. So I give you that permission. I'm using my authority to grant you authority to do that which welcomes God's people."

That trust and freedom can spread into a whole congregation. My community has asked me to take on this authority as a priest, to be the one who orders worship. I use that authority to say to everyone around me, "This liturgy is our work, the work of the people. Now you get to listen closely to where God is calling us, and to bring that wisdom and insight to light in the worship that we all share."

# CHAPTER 9

# Do Unto Others

SHANE CLAIBORNE (in person)

**How do you go from becoming high school prom king to becoming an ordinary radical?**

> *Shane Claiborne:* I did a dangerous thing of reading the Bible, and asking what if Jesus meant this stuff he said. And found a group of people that sort of allowed me to think that maybe he did. I'm still recovering from all the sexism, and racism, and everything I grew up with.

**I can't think of a single prophet that went "Yippee" when they were called by God.**

> *Shane Claiborne:* That's definitely been the case for us. The way that I've chosen only seems sacrificial because of where I've come from, but I don't think that what we're doing is anything other than what ordinary Christianity has looked like throughout history, starting with Mary and Martha.

**Contrast all of this to the fact that the wealthiest, most powerful country in the world is also the most depressed and medicated.**

> *Shane Claiborne:* I believe that salvation in the sense of a *salve* or a *healing balm* comes through community and relationship. It's almost impossible for that healing to happen in isolation. That's where I would say Jesus loved and cared about the rich and powerful and that's why he invited them to the margins to live and see love at work. I see lonely

rich people over and over, who are in these compartmentalized worlds, come to life in the city, as they play with fire hydrants, go to block parties, meet folks that are homeless, and give of themselves. I think there is a secret hunch that if Jesus loves these people like that then he must love me, too.

**You guys have been called theological pranksters.**

*Shane Claiborne:* I think there are ways of stirring up good questions around things that are happening without confronting it directly head-on. That's what Jesus was brilliant at doing. They ask him, "Hey, do you pay your taxes?" He pulled the coin out of a fish's mouth. Also, he didn't ride a donkey in the Passover because he was a Democrat. He was showing everybody that he was a different kind of king. It's so weird, but he's always transcending those categories and questions.

**Some folks who preach that kind of tolerance, love, and justice are so durn angry.**

*Shane Claiborne:* I've been arrested fifteen or twenty times, but it's always been amid people who were marked by gentleness and doing things that reflected Christ. The police officers that arrested us feeding people in Love Park in Philly said, "You have such a gentle spirit." They came to court to argue the charges they charged us with be dropped. That's the place I really want to be where we celebrate something different rather than just protesting.

## ♟ BRIAN McLAREN (in person)

**Why are you the chairman of the board for Sojourners/Call to Renewal?**

*Brian McLaren:* Over the twenty-four years I was a pastor, I watched our climate change in the US, so that the word Christian and the name Jesus meant something different in 2007 than they did in say 1974. I realized what had happened was that the Religious Right had very successfully mobilized evangelicals around a certain set of political issues, and they had employed a certain set of political and rhetorical strategies to do so. What that meant for me as a pastor was that the words had been poisoned. They had taken on a kind of culture-war connotation. In recent years Sojourners' message started getting a hearing to help change the impression of what it means to be a Christian, what it means to say I believe in Jesus. In a sense, they began breaking the monopoly of the Religious Right in defining the most important terms of our faith. I really liked what they were doing and I approached them and one thing led to another.

**What can we in the West learn from the churches in the global south?**

*Brian McLaren:* There's a lot wrong with us, and we have a lot of blind spots, so we need to listen to our brothers and sisters around the world. One of the problems is that it's actually hard to hear the voices of our brothers and sisters from the global south, because the voices that come through to us via the media and other filters tend to be those voices that echo what we already think. For example, Christians in Latin America working with the poor have a lot to say to us regarding poverty. But it's not easy to hear those voices, because the prosperity gospel preachers in Latin America—who echo our prosperity televangelists here—are the ones who get on the air. That means that we have to put in special effort to read the writings of non-Western theologians. It means we need to go on mission trips not just to preach and teach, but to listen and learn—not just to evangelize, but to be evangelized.

## ✉ KESTER BREWIN (e-mail)

**What are some of the unique challenges to doing urban ministry?**

*Kester Brewin:* Facing "the other." In the city there are just so many people, the potentiality for relationship is so high . . . and thus the potentiality for getting hurt is so high. So people are excited about being in the city, but also guarded. They are also so busy, and so used to spectacles. You can't stun people into belief. You have to work slowly—more slowly than you would probably have to in a rural context.

**Where do you find hints of God in the city?**

*Kester Brewin:* Everywhere. There is no place where God can't be found. Even in the places that seem God-less, they are full of God for that—full of God's ache to pull people there and do something.

**Why do you say that the city is the place where our dreamy theologies must get their hands dirty and work themselves out in praxis?**

*Kester Brewin:* Because too often we see academic theology doing very little to actually impact practice on the ground. It's too top down.

Good theology starts with dirty hands and a good heart, and works out the tidy thoughts later. If you start with pure reason, you'll never get your heart fully enough involved to get down and change things.

**How do you see churches engaging in issues of social justice without becoming political pawns?**

*Kester Brewin:* By not being impressed with power, not finding power attractive. Too often churches have had political influence dangled in front of them by the powerful—and been tempted by the thought that if they just compromised this once and got involved at that level they could do so much more. It's never worked. Instead, they should just keep fighting away at the coal face: highlighting injustice and working to stamp it out from the bottom up, not the top down.

## ✉ KURT NEILSON (e-mail)

**What prompted your interest in establishing a ministry to prostitutes?**

*Kurt Neilson:* I was exposed to a rich ministry of outreach to people in the sex trade in Chicago: Catholic Theological Union partnered with a group of people practicing a "ministry of presence" to folk in prostitution on the North Side. Edwina Gately and De Paul Genska (the latter a Franciscan Friar) led groups of students on "the stroll" after hours to pick-up bars and places where the women and their pimps and johns hung out. They all went on to found "Genesis House," a long-term residence for women trying to "get out of the life." Years later, here in Portland, the women were our neighbors, turning tricks right on the church property corners. It was a matter of asking "who is our neighbor?" and trying to respond.

**What have you learned about God from your ministry with prostitutes?**

*Kurt Neilson:* Persons in prostitution inhabit a world not our own, with different rules, different sense of time and place, different view of life and persons and genders. In many ways this view is witheringly honest—they see the disillusioning truth in their customers, many of whom occupy "respectable" places in the day-world (in schools, churches, law enforcement, and every other aspect of society). They mirror both the determination of the human person to survive as well as the frailties of all with whom they deal. And they reveal as well the truth of our culture, which in some measure relies upon people serving the sex trade in a way similar to how our whole economy relies upon the impoverishment and exploitation of other people the world over. This is hard and painful and humiliating to hear, but hear it we must.

**What advice would you offer for anyone who feels called to start a similar ministry?**

*Kurt Neilson:* Dream and imagine, call on the Holy Ones, the ancient saints, to come and make a home. Take their lives as example and their prayers and presence as strength. Tell, tell the vision to others and watch the eyes in which it is enkindled and nurture those flames.

## ISAAC EVERETT (in person)

**How do you see Transmission as an outreach ministry?**

*Isaac Everett:* We're kind of a motley group. We have people that grew up atheist, Episcopalian, Lutheran, Catholic, evangelical, and one person who was born into Transmission (although he's only four months old). Some people view Transmission as their primary community, others see it as a supplement to traditional church—I think both are fine. Transmission really isn't about gaining numbers. Some people view evangelism as saving souls and I'm not into that at all. The salvation I experience in Christ is salvation from the loneliness and apathy that is so prevalent in secular New York culture. Jesus declares that power, wealth, and status aren't the most important goals, and that reality is the outreach that Transmission offers us. Transmission helps people discover the richness of a life lived in community and the joy of a life dedicated to justice, peace, and love.

**Any final words?**

*Isaac Everett:* Fight the power. Don't do anything half-assed.

## Easter for the Outcasts

From God's Politics blog, http://blog.beliefnet.com/godspolitics/2007/03/becky-garrison-easter-for-outcasts.html, March 26, 2007

*Becky Garrison:* As expected, I get a lot of Christian press releases around Christmas and Easter. Most of the material gets circular filed under "been there, done that;" "would love to attend, but I have too many other Christian commitments;" or "Christ died and rose for THIS?" But this year, I got a press release titled "Church, Artists and Sex Workers plan an Experiential Easter Service," that piqued my curiosity.

Transmission, an underground Manhattan church, is working with sex workers and artists to celebrate Mary Magdalene's role in the gospel resurrection story, her personal relationship with Jesus, her witness on behalf of the risen Christ, and contemporary sex worker issues. They chose Mary Magdalene because Christ appeared to her before anyone else and entrusted her with the news of his resurrection although the other apostles didn't believe her (Matthew 28:1–10; Mark 16:1–11; Luke 24:1–10; and John 20:1–18).

While some Christians call Mary Magdalene a prostitute, or say she was the woman caught in the act of adultery (John 8:3–11), a careful reading will reveal these are later interpretations of the text as the institutionalized church marginalized her and concocted stories of her being a prostitute. Rather than give this story a Gnostic update, Transmission appears to be going back to the Bible basics to explore, on Easter Sunday, the significant role this allegedly fallen woman played in helping to spread the gospel.

Throughout his ministry, Jesus surrounded himself with those who society had rejected as outcasts and undesirables. "In my experience," says Transmission co-founder Bowie Snodgrass, "listening to sex workers tell their stories can blow the lids off morally-loaded religious debates about sex and economics, revealing deep human truths, lives, complexities, and questions." What does it mean to have a service that welcomes all but makes an effort to target those whom society has shunned as unclean and undesirable?

Jesus welcomed all into his kingdom, teaching us that we are all equal in God's eyes, and as such we are equally worthy of being loved. According to Transmission's Web site, "All are welcome regardless of age, gender, profession, or the number of times they've been born."

The venue for this service is Club Avalon, formerly known as the notorious New York nightclub Limelight. Originally, this gothic revival structure was built as Holy Communion Episcopal Church by William Augustus Muhlenberg, who later instituted a radical ministry to help brothel workers and abandoned mistresses start new lives. He earned a place on the Episcopal calendar of feasts and fasts, the Anglican equivalent of being made a saint. Coincidentally, Easter Sunday happens to fall on his Feast Day. Coincidence? You decide.

Instead of having a clergyperson lead and direct the entire thing, every member of Transmission will play a part in guiding the worship experience. The service will include performance poetry, modern dance, graffiti art, a live band playing Madonna covers, and much, much more. "Rather than directing ritual activity," says Isaac Everett, "we're creating an interactive environment which will allow people to connect with the Easter story on their own terms and at their own pace. It's important to us that everyone who comes has an access point, regardless of who they are." Collaborators on this venture include members of PONY (Prostitutes Organization of New York), artists from Storahtelling (a Jewish ritual theater company), and local seminarians.

I've worshipped with Isaac Everett on and off for several years now and I can attest to the power of his music. This is no free-for-all, anything-goes kind of service, but a service that will be grounded by Isaac's love of liturgy and the Word, as well as his skill as a music worship leader. I just found out that his work will be distributed by Jonny Baker's Proost label. I've worked with Jonny enough to know that it's well worth checking out his new resources that fuel faith.

Even though my Easter Sunday tends to be booked solid, something tells me I should carve out a bit of space and check out this service. For those who are in the New York City area, come join me on Sunday, April 8, starting at 6 p.m. in Club Avalon, 47 West 20th Street (at Sixth Avenue). No cover charge, just come as you are. I have no idea what to expect—but then again, neither did Mary Magdalene when she first went to the tomb.

## ☎ PAIGE BLAIR (phone)

**Elaborate on how you decided to connect the U2charist services to the Millennium Development Goals.**

*Paige Blair:* U2 has been involved in efforts to eradicate poverty since the Live Aid Concert in 1985, and their lyrics often have a social justice edge, coupled with Bono's work with the One Campaign. Also, there are no restraints so long as all the money is going to UN Millennium Development Goals charities.

**How do you see worship as a vehicle for social justice?**

*Paige Blair:* As we pray in Eucharist prayer C, we come to this table not "for solace only but for strength, not for pardon only, but for renewal." If we've done our job through the liturgy, then when we're told to go forth "to love and serve the Lord," we can go out and be cocreators with God and do his work in the world.

**How do you see churches engaging in issues of social justice without becoming political pawns?**

*Paige Blair:* The Millennium Development Goals along with The One campaign is a bipartisan movement. If either party is missing the boat on social justice, then they need to ask why.

*Stop asking God to bless what you're doing.*
*Get involved in what God is doing—*
*because it's already blessed."*

—Bono, National Prayer Breakfast (February 2, 2006)

# KAREN WARD:
## The Missional Church in Action

👤 KAREN WARD (in person)

*Karen Ward:* I was born and bred in the mainline church, and worked in the ELCA headquarters in Chicago in two departments, ecumenical affairs and later in the worship office. The church is my home and these are my people.

The Church of the Apostles (COTA) was a dream that was partly fueled by CCM, the "Call to Common Mission," which is a joint Lutheran-Episcopal full communion agreement. Some opponents of the agreement made a joke calling CCM "necrophilia," two declining churches embracing each other in death. Yet our Seattle area Lutheran and Episcopal bishops decided, Okay. Let's show the naysayers that CCM is not about hierarchy, and what better way than to have a "common mission baby" together? So, they had a baby mission, and that was us.

To tell the truth, I have always been a 'closeted' Anglican. Recently, I've come out of this closet to embrace my true identity in the sunshine and fresh air. In the UK, Anglicanism emerging groups are called "fresh expressions." This fits COTA more than most know.

Now more than ever, I'm very excited to do more speaking and teaching about the amazing "convergence" we experience at COTA between Anglican ethos and practice and the ethos and practice of the emerging church.

We have a passion to speak to our "tribes" as we call them. I believe that our spiritual heritage and the DNA of our Anglican and Lutheran traditions are very much worth preserving, enlivening, and passing on to the next tradition. If we don't do it, nobody is going to do this for us.

I wish the wider church would step out of its myopia and see the power that's going on. They get so bogged down in modernistic battles between liberals and conservatives that they don't see the forest for the trees. While I'm very aware of what's going on in the wider Episcopal Church, we're not in a crisis at COTA. We're just having a great old time diving around in the Anglican tradition and finding all kinds of great resources to faith, life, and hope.

We are "free-range" and out there exploring the contours of faith in our postmodern culture. Bishop Warner had a meeting with me and he said, "Well Karen, I don't understand everything that you're going to be doing, but I think your approach will be able to reach out to a lot of younger people that we haven't been able to communicate with." Then he said, "You're going to have a very long leash from the diocese." I looked at him and I said, "Bishop, no leash." There was silence. But then he got it.

Basically, we are off leash. We have been blessed and released. Many don't totally understand our expressions of music and liturgy, but they love us. They trust us running off leash because we are very oriented to the diocese as "home." There's something about a child that has the trust of their parents. When you know that your parents trust you, you behave in a trustworthy manner.

Before we had a permanent space, we were on the go in the diocese having services in nightclubs, coffee houses, and wherever. We had an idea about having a service at the diocesan house. They actually gave us the keys to this mansion on the historical register. It was like giving us the keys to the family car. There were some raised eyebrows on the diocesan council with thoughts of off leash Apostles running amuck in the diocesan house. But again, they decided to trust us, maybe because we had a trustworthy track record so far (and meaning the Holy Spirit still on the job).

I deal with our young Apostles in the same manner as the diocese deals with us. They know that I trust them and because I trust them, they act trustworthy. Our Apostles are mostly in their twenties. So, I feel like a den mother. But we are getting more intergenerational, as we're now attracting people in their sixties, some of whom are the parents of these twentysomethings. Also, we've had some babies born to the community.

What we try to teach at COTA is the methodology of contextualization and being incarnational. I hate to use the word "model," but there are about five or six models that can work within a traditional Anglican context. The church within a church strategy is effective in England with communities such as Moot and Grace in London. We're not like that, but we are all very attached to the Anglican world.

Another way that's underused is for an established church to "adopt" an emerging mission. That's a way to pass on the DNA. A traditional church that wants to grow, and learn, and change can put themselves "in relationship" with a mission that they would sponsor. For example, the Cathedral Church of St. Paul in Boston is sponsoring us this year by giving us $3,000. We went there to lead a "learning party" event on emerging church and mission. We go around the country and do these workshops in any diocese that will let us in.

At the learning party at Boston Stephanie Spellers came with about five or six people that she had been talking with about doing something. Shortly after we left, they got inspired and formed their pre-existing group to be more organized to do things. Then they sent someone here to COTA to observe us. The Crossings, a new congregation "of" the Cathedral Church of St. Paul, was born.

Also, new church plants can be started. This is the most effective way emerging church DNA is most concentrated in groups that are ground up, emerging as "total churches" (rather than groups within already modern structured churches). We have to create new emerging forms of everything, from kid's ministry to church governance, to teaching stewardship . . . all of which traditional churches can observe and learn from.

While we get funding from other churches, we're not under the authority of any church. It's harder, but you get a more pure strain because you're not introducing two strains of DNA into the mix and hoping it catches. A church may think they want to give birth to a church plant, but once it arrives and changes the parents' DNA, they may react. It may cause a virus or an antibody reaction when this new strain is introduced.

We're now helping with a baby church plant named Church of the Beloved, in Edmonds, Washington. Technically, Beloved is an ECLA plant. Ryan Marsh, age twenty-eight, who was our Curate of Liturgical Arts for three years, is heading that up. He was interested in the Episcopal Church, but they didn't have a "pioneer ministry" track similar to the Church of England. But the ELCA has started something they call "TEEM" (theological education for emerging ministries) so that's why he went through the ELCA instead of the Episcopal Church.

Sometimes I think we fascinate the diocese. I've heard, "Oh those Apostles. You never know what they're going to do!" We get busloads of youth groups from various mainline denominations coming, so at first some of our folk were kind of joking, "We ought to sell tickets. Come to an emerging service and get a deal on pizza across the street." But I put a stop to that, I said, "People are dropping off their kids at our doorstep. This is amazing and something very significant. They're trusting us with their children." Then, they saw this as a God-given ministry for us to host young people, who have hopes and dreams about having more of a voice in their own traditional church back home. Sometimes they have to come to Apostles to see somebody else doing what they want to do in their own parish. We've had people from all over the country, Europe, and even Africa. We bless them and send them back to their communities with hope.

A tamer model is to simply do an alternate worship service in a traditional church. It will take much longer to impact the parent church's DNA, but it's a start.

However, I find there's a "freedom in poverty." We don't have a dime often and live literally "month-to-month." So we have huge freedom, but it comes with a price. Our church has been filled with twentysomethings for a while, but it's filled with people who don't have much money. Our goal is to be self-sustainable and we're about three years away from that goal.

We're adapting a "new monastic" ethos here. We see how monks and nuns are self-sustaining. One of the things we're doing is exploring how the monks and nuns take care of themselves. They make candles, beer, or rosaries, they run retreat houses. We have four "house church" micro communities resonate with "Catholic Worker" model, with up to four live-in "monks" in the Abbey, a St. Brigit House apartment for interns and pilgrims, a COTA community Rule of Life (which is not just for our "residential monastics" but for our entire church community, as we are basically approaching church as a new monastic "3rd order parish" with an "abbey," church), and monastic cottage industries, where we make prayer beads and host pilgrims.

As the Roman church has many different orders each with a different vibe and focus, contemporary monasticism has many "charisms" focuses and expressions. The UK Anglican emerging groups tend to be more "new Benedictine," while the most well known of the United States groups tend to be "new Franciscan."

Our COTA form is 'new wave Benedictine,' which is chilled, ambient and "quiet." We do serious *ora et labora* (prayer/liturgy and work) as a focus but in our own neighborhood and sustained by daily prayer, weekly Eucharist and contemplation on the mysteries of God. Our communities work is consistent, regular, parochial, and pastoral like a computer processor's 'subroutines' running quiet, yet deep rather than being overtly radical, whereas traveling to be with the poor in Calcutta or being bombed in Iraq is very radical and Franciscan.

Right now, we want to buy the old 1914 closed down urban church that we call the "Fremont Abbey" that currently houses the Apostles. To raise the money, we're going to try selling CDs and running a café. We are socially responsible and will sell organic fair trade coffee and tea and we are co-op partnering with our nonprofit Fremont Abbey

Arts Center to earn enough funds to sustain our mission and ministry. But first we have to put in a commercial kitchen, update the electrical system, get sprinklers, an elevator, and take on other major start-up costs to retrofit our beloved, old abbey into a thriving nonprofit café and arts center and mission hub for Church of the Apostles.

This neighborhood is becoming a gentrified district as people move back into the city. It's now filled with younger people (20s–30s) and new $700,000 condos. Everywhere is "commercialized hospitality" offered by Starbucks and bars with $10 martinis, which offers a kind of community, but only for a certain class and with a certain "price" that many can't afford. Fremont Baptist Church and COTA are the only two remaining churches in this neighborhood of approximately 20,000 people. We're the only spaces that are preserved for the public good. Here the homeless and the yuppies can come in and get a cup of coffee. We need to preserve this human space that's available to diverse communities before it becomes all commercialized. But given the rise in rents, it's been a fight for us to raise money to help us buy back this church. The diocese and has committed to raise $100,000 and we have to raise $205,000.

One of the problems we face in funding is that in today's modern church's system for grant making, where innovation is not rewarded over time, as in the "nonchurch world" of start-ups. As long as we have good ideas and good projects that meet grant agency goals, why not keep funding us, and whoever else has similar projects? In the "real world," the venture capital and funds are given based on good ideas, so if you have many good ideas you can obtain many allocations of funding over time.

We have a young adult spiritual formation grant for three years from Trinity Church Wall Street, that's the basics for our work. In this grant we focused on Ancient-Future Common Prayer. The next part phase we will do is Ancient-Future Spiritual Formation, based on the baptismal covenant lived out in live work community houses similar to those of Dorothy Day and the Catholic Worker movement for young adults and others wanting to connect the baptismal covenant to daily life. Yet part two probably can't be funded because it doesn't fall within current grant guidelines of giving two grants to one group. We're doing it anyway, because that's what we do, and this is our calling. We already have three houses—Brigit, Ikon and Praxis—which we struggle to keep going due to lack of funds, so pray for a way for grant rules to be changed and for the 815 to begin to see fund mission innovators, so we

**151**

have help to move forward with new mission initiative that will bring great learning and benefit to the whole Episcopal Church.

Another program we came up with is the "Anglican Missioner Exchange" program. We've had about seven Brits come over to visit COTA for a couple of weeks for a month. This is a great cross-fertilization where we exchange ideas and inspire each other. We got a $5,000 grant from the Evangelical Education Society and sent one of our priests over to England for a month to work at Moot and St. Matthews. He came back all fired up. We want to set up a program where we set up short-term exchanges of up to three months and create a Church of England and US Episcopal Church exchange. These entrepreneurial missioners can swap DNA. We could expand this to Canada, Australia, New Zealand—this project has a lot of potential. The US–UK exchange is happening informally, but so far the wider church isn't learning what we're discovering because there's no funding to document the findings, make videos, pay for plane tickets.

I know there are some nut fringes out there that talk about "emergence." They put out some coffee and candles and call it emerging. That's not what this is about. Also, a lot of these guys are still struggling with sexuality and female issues. The Brits are a lot more theologically erudite than the Americans on this. That's why at the Apostles, we hang out with Brits more than anybody. They've been doing this since the 1980s, and are pretty advanced with this emerging dialogue. There's a lot of British material that should be read here in the US but it isn't.

As emerging Episcopalians, we get lonely. I find going to Greenbelt is akin to getting a shot in the arm. We get to see our peers and we're all crazy and connect together.

To do this work you need to have people with integrity and authenticity, who are postmodern doing this stuff. You can't fake this stuff, though some folks may try.

I tend to laugh at these "certificate" programs. Instead, we just go and we spend time with people. Also, we exchange ideas and critique each other online. I'll tell Jonny Baker that a given idea is a bunch of crap or whatever. We all can give validity to each other. If you want to know if I'm legitimate, ask three people that you know are legit. If they all tell you I'm legit, I'm legit. It's a cross reference of relationality similar to the early church, where Paul commends Timothy to the church he is sending him to.

I try to find authentic voices and support them with everything that I have. For instance, when Jonny sends me someone, I know they're authentic because I've built a relationship with Jonny and we trust each other.

I have a lot in common with my evangelical emergent brethren and we meet in the Emergent Village, but we're coming from different starting points. The mainliners and evangelicals are building bridges from the other side. We may meet in the middle, but we're attending to our side of it.

Sometimes I see people saying, "Oh I want one of those accessories" as though emerging church is a cute play toy. But if there's nothing authentic behind it, it'll fade away because no one has their heart around what's going on. Somebody actually called me up and said, "We heard you were a hip new thing. What do you guys do?" I said, "We just baptized a baby, we married a couple. We're a church. What do you think we do? We preach the Gospel, we minister the sacraments, we console the brokenhearted, we instruct the wayward. We're a church. We're not playing 'cool worship.'" They were looking at us for techniques that they could use. Yeah we have cool media, but the point is not that we have cool media. This is authentic to us because this is stuff that our young people do themselves. They happen to be of the i-Pod generation. So we're not doing it to be cool, we're doing it to be authentic to who we are.

One of our sister churches is Saints Peter and Paul Episcopal Church in Portland, Oregon. They're an Anglo-Catholic traditional church with a Celtic spirituality and yet they're dealing with prostitutes. We think they're every bit as much of an emerging church as us. What we have in common is our authenticity, not that we look alike.

If I ever became a bishop, all hell (or heaven) would break loose. There are so many young people out there that have no freedom. I just would like to open the floodgates to them to bless and release them, believing in them to be responsible, trustworthy, and able to lead us into God's future with hope.

## Anglican Communion Facetime "Anglimerges"

From Karen Ward's blog, Submerge (http://submerge.typepad.com/submergence/2007/07/true-anglican-c.html), July 23, 2007

*Karen Ward:* I've been focused much these days on the Anglican Communion and all the goings on with fears surrounding a breach. Even so, some of us will remain grounded by a theology of *commun-*

**153**

*ion* that is *un-breakable* because it is *perichoretic* and thus needs to be *proleptic* within the church.

So I started a Facebook group called "Anglimergent," to give this kind of *communion* theology some good old Anglican incarnation/ embodiment in cyberspace and hopefully in physical space also into the future.

The whole idea is to engage emerging church "conversation" across divides and *within* the Anglican communion. If such conversations among diverse friends can yield fruit among vastly different Christian traditions within the wider emerging church conversation, then emergent conversation can also help us image and incarnate an alternate Anglican future that is different from the breach scenario and "Anglican family feud."

We are supposed to see Christ in the "other," so Anglimergent is trying to give some face and talk time to diverse Anglicans seeking missonal unity and friendship (TEC, AMiA, CANA, ACC, CofE, the Anglican Church of Uganda . . .) to show that God can indeed be found in the face of whoever is seen as Anglican "Others."

My dream is for there to be an Anglimergent Cafe Space at the next General Convention in 2009.

# CHAPTER 10

# Moving Forward

**How do you see technology (blogs, podcasts) as tools to advance the gospel?**

> *Spencer Burke (phone):* Everything is moving from analog to digital and they function in a radically different way. We're moving from a postal community to an e-mail community. A postal community is a top down community where we decide who can carry the mail, and what's happened within this community is that they were getting competition from places you never knew this would happen such as FedEx and DHL. We can pump more and more money into the postal systems we love, or we can ask the question about working on a more radically different system. In an e-mail world, people educate themselves, people take chances and they fail. They socially network rather than a top down gain. The problem is you have no control over these messages that go in and out, not to mention problems with viruses and spam.
>
> This independent world breeds interdependence. The abuse of power and funding is going to be microscopic because none of these smaller groups will get over forty-nine people. When we count up the number of times people are volunteering at places that aren't church branded or giving 5 or 10 bucks to a person who needs money or literally taking someone into their home, all of those dollars or hours are gifts to the church of God in the name of Jesus loving the poor and oppressed, but it won't show up anywhere on any church budget. Does the right hand need to know what the left hand is doing? I don't need to have it printed up in our church bulletin how much was given to God this week.

One Sunday our family went down to a convalescent home, a month before we went to a local park and just hung out with people who wouldn't have had a meal otherwise. Sometimes we go to a church that's a few hours long with some very interesting worship. My kids and I and my wife are listening to some very interesting sermons on our iPod. Then there's a local church here that we gather and commune with but not on a weekly basis.

*Nadia Bolz-Weber (e-mail):* I wonder if there should be a Hippocratic Oath for Christians. "At first, do the Gospel no harm." Technology is neutral. The intentionality around its use is what makes it work for good or evil. Here's my *opinion*: a room full of worshipers who stare for an hour at a huge video screen (not unlike the rest of their lives) with Tom Cruise film clips and vapid "Jesus is my Boyfriend" lyrics: evil. A room full of worshippers who are focused on the central symbols of the faith, perhaps some of which are occasionally on a screen: good. I cannot stress enough that this is an example of my own sinful, narrow opinions and should not in anyway be taken as authoritative in the least (although don't get me wrong, I'm totally right about this).

I'm a big fan of the blog. When I started Sarcastic Lutheran: The Cranky Spirituality of a Postmodern Gal–Emerging Church ala Luther, I seriously thought that perhaps up to half a dozen of my friends would read it and mostly out of loyalty. I'm shocked to report that thousands of people from all over the world read the thing, many of whom e-mail me with messages like "thank you so much, I thought I was the only one who thought like this." Now I see my blog as a ministry, a little piece of the Internet for the lunatic fringe of the church. Being part of the emerging church blogosphere has led me to develop amazing friendships with folks in the UK, Australia, and all over the states, most of whom I've now met. I pray daily for 9 churches, 3 of which are in England. I'm connected to them through both low and high tech means: prayer and the web . . . the prayer part is just as central as the checking their blogs part.

*Ian Mobsby says (IM chat):* OK—postmodernism can be interpreted as a return to the narrative and metaphor—so that the stories of Christ and metaphor such as the parables have a new place in engagement with the culture—therefore a relational approach—where blogs and website enable communication through dispersed relationships—then the gospels can be communicated in relational, narrative, and metaphorical form.

*Ian Mobsby says:* this relates to my comments relating to new forms of mysticism coming out of contemporary culture . . . so it enables new forms of relating—so not new forms of cold evangelism—but more gentle forms of engagement with Christian spirituality.

*Marilyn Haskel (phone):* If the church ignores this whole technology growth, they're not going to last long. There are ways to use it in the church and people will discover this as they move along. Does this mean that at some point we might not have a printed book, but everyone will have a screen like they do at Jet Blue and follow the service? I know that projecting music on the wall on a screen no longer feels foreign to many congregations nowadays. You do need to ask if you're doing this to be relevant or get at truth wherever it can be found. If people are grounded in their beliefs and know why they believe what they believe but open to change. Change is frightening. Fear plays incredible role in all of our lives as Christians. I enjoy and like change. So, I find that when I've had to make a decision, if I wait and discern long enough and watch the signs and hear what I believe is God's speaking to me in my prayer life, that's all I can do. I trust that that's going to work.

*Kurt Neilson (e-mail):* Hey, was it Malcolm X in a very different context who said "by any means necessary"? It's not my skill as of yet, but I know that if we are serious about engaging real people that we must engage them where they themselves engage themselves, one another, and the world. Did I say "they"? I meant "we"!

You know, I think that future experience of community, worship, evangelism, etc. will be a startling mixture of "high" and "low" tech. Drums, human chant, burning incense and candles, spoken stories by a live storyteller, face-to-face community will always have a place, perhaps even more of a place if and when people experience the alienating aspects of contemporary technology. Me, I don't think a computer screen adequately replaces gazing into someone's eyes. But maybe I'm a fossil (did I say "maybe"?).

*Phyllis Tickle (in person):* We've got to recognize that more and more people are doing their private worship using the Internet in one way or another. And let us not forget that we can also get rid of a lot of organizational hoopla using the Internet. There is such a thing as a virtual community. No small part of its appeal, by the way, is that the Internet invites a kind of intimacy that maybe many of us don't even get face to face.

*Brian McLaren (in person):* Because there is so much explosion of new technology—it's a good time for us to go back to the writings of Marshall McLuhan, the philosopher of technology. Shane Hipps recently wrote a book that tries to make McLuhan's thought accessible to church leaders. McLuhan said that every innovation is an amputation For example, when you invent the wheel, your legs become weaker. When you invent the television, your ability to become present becomes weaker. When you invent the amplifier, your voice becomes weaker. We need to reflect on this powerful insight and ask, In what ways is technology subtracting or amputating just at the moment we think it's adding and empowering? We should always use it with care, remembering that Jesus modeled personal incarnation, not projection and amplification.

I don't know exactly what impact the Internet will have on the local church, for example, but it will have an impact in many areas, including education. Internet-based people know that information is ubiquitous, and they feel empowered to seek it out. They don't need you to spoon-feed them information in lectures like the used to; they can Google it way faster. They need you to do other things . . . to help them sift through the information, integrate it, incarnate it, reflect on it, model it.

In view of technology, the question remains what is it that the gathered church can do that nobody else can do? I think there are exciting answers to that question and those answers can help clarify our role in ministry in the years to come.

*Jonny Baker (e-mail):* They are simply that—tools for communication. They should be used by people who are at home in that environment. Marshall Macluhan writes how new technologies get used by people from the old world to do what the old technologies did rather than something new. So the danger for churches is that they use podcasts and blogs to publish services and sermons rather than exploring the opportunities the new media afford. Positively I see technology is about furthering relationships and networks, self-publishing, connectivity, creativity, and participation. Negative factors are the danger of being exclusive, information overload, security (of data and people—e.g., children), spam, pornography, and the fuelling of the consumer dream where me and my good taste are at the world's centre.

*Cheryl Lawrie (phone):* Only have blogs or podcasts if you have something to say. Technology shouldn't be automatic tool. It isolates and divides communities as much as it brings us together. We have to get more savvy about how we use these tools. If you make your website look attractive and professional, people trust it. I think that's dangerous. We need to be much more discerning than ever before about our sources of wisdom.

*Kevin Goodrich (e-mail):* While we should use these means of communication to advance the gospel, there's a value of being unplugged. Many of the seeker churches are polished to high performance. Here in North Dakota, we get close to nature and say that it's ok to dial out of technology and be the organic beings that God created us to be.

*Kevin Bean (in person):* Obviously nothing beats personal interaction, but at St. Bart's we have also established a regional, even national, presence. We're not looking to be a cyber congregation per se, but we are exploring how we can take the conversations we're having here to a broader realm. That includes for example, when we posted on our website a sermon I preached that resulted in my catching holy hell as it were from people as far away at South Carolina and Arkansas, because I took a strong open and affirming stance on issues of sexual orientation. So I had a great chance to do some really interactive stuff with folks. Then there's blogging, though one of the downsides of blogging is that there will always be people who will take a thing you're saying and blow it out of proportion. It brings out the snipers as well as the thoughtful responses. But web-based technology is now an essential tool in church growth, and in connecting with the wider world.

*Kester Brewin (e-mail):* They can facilitate communications between and among these groups. What they can't do is replicate them. No matter how good the technology, you cannot mediate presence. And I don't believe you ever will. Blogging will settle down. There's currently too much noise . . . too many people talking for it really to be called a conversation. It will develop more toward this—better tools for conversations between nodes, rather than nodes just mouthing off into the aether.

*Peter Rollins (phone):* Experimenting with changing Ikon's website to a Wiki (http://www.mediawiki.org/wiki/MediaWiki) allows us to experiment with a communal hermeneutic. We're trying to say we encourage people in the entire community to interact with each other and interpret our faith together.

*Page Blair (phone):* Scholarship in the late 1990s went into how the Gospel of Mark was written as if it was an ancient Greek novel. It was done this way because the evangelist wanted to be sure people read it. So they used a medium that was acceptable to the people they were trying to reach. Archbishop Thomas Crammer believed it was really important that people be able to worship in the vernacular, hence the Book of Common Prayer in English. So, podcasts, PowerPoint presentations, U2 Eucharists and so on are all part of an ancient tradition of sharing the good news in a way that the people who need to hear the story will hear the story.

We're going to see more and more churches with wireless Internet access. Churches that can't afford full-time clergy and don't feel connected to the diocese could download a podcast of the bishop's service every week. So, churches could be connected in a way they haven't been connected before. But the one thing that the sermon at home can't offer is contact with other human beings through which we can experience God's love.

*Isaac Everett (in person):* When the gospel was translated into German and people could read the Bible for themselves, it changed theology and it changed the church. Blogs and podcasts are doing similar things; they're leveling the playing field and allowing anyone to be published. Authority and influence aren't mediated commodities anymore.

**How do you define church in the twenty-first century?**

*Phyllis Tickle (in person):* Church is a community of believers who come together to mentor and disciple each other for that thing which is the incarnating of the gospel right where you are. Only church can do that. The church is people and community. It's all the little pieces of us coming together to be the big body of God on earth.

*Catherine Roskam (in person):* It's the ecclesia, as it was in the early church—the gathering of the people of God. We can cast that net wide and include a lot of people, who more and more in the midst of our culture's rampant consumerism long for spiritual food. I do think despite the conventional wisdom, a denomination does make a difference, and I think the Episcopal church is particularly well equipped to preach the gospel in our current context, offering a reasonable and holy alternative to the polar opposites of atheism and fundamentalism that seem to have captured the public conversation, at least on the Internet. Our common worship is central to our identity and also to our mission.

*Brian McLaren (in person):* The term I like to use is deep ecclesiology (a term my tall skinny Kiwi friend Andrew Jones created). If we made a list of church bodies from the most hierarchical and historic "high churches" down through the mid-range of state churches and historic denominations and then low-church congregations, nondenominational or independent churches, house churches and storefront churches, and so on . . . we see a range of expression. The history of Protestantism has in a sense been the story of downward mobility, culminating in this last one hundred years of the worldwide Pentecostal explosion. Now, in emerging churches, there are new forms of church being explored—and the downward expansion continues. In the past, though, we constantly argue over which churches within the bandwidth were legitimate churches. Now, we need to honor the church in all its forms, to appreciate it at all its levels, and realize that all forms of church have a role to play in mission. There's plenty of sin and injustice to go around, you know?

*Peter Rollins (phone):* That's a tough one. I guess I will say this, however: in the West I think we will continue to rediscover the wealth of the mystical tradition and negative theology. These are the wells that we should drink from and which may bring new life to the church. I really hope we rediscover the place of parable, of art, of not trying to give people doctrinal answers but rather to evoke questions. In Ikon we are exploring the idea of transformative art, an art form that evokes transformation in the participant. My hope is that there will be a place for this transformance art in the wider church body sometime in the future.

*Jonny Baker (e-mail):* The body of Christ down the ages and across the world. Its local expressions should be hugely diverse.

*Spencer Burke (phone):* I think we need more heretics to challenge the systems that exist and try to listen to what these people are saying rather than write them off. I think we will find church in these amazing and beautiful ways—I hope that the institutional church would not think they are the final answer, but they would grow and evolve. I don't think the house church is the answer and I'm not anti-megachurch. My dissent is not based on opportunism but love for the church itself. The church will continue to exist, but I don't think the institutional church will exist.

But if we can find out what brings us together rather than what separates us, we can transcend the old conversations. There are public and private voices, and even though people think I'm on the right track with so many things, they have a constituency and as long as money, power, and prestige are involved in these things, we're all kind of screwed.

*Isaac Everett (in person):* Our church needs to connect with our culture or else our culture is going to leave our church behind. Allowing us to worship in our own cultural context not only makes worship more coherent, it also affirms the presence of God in our culture. We can be who we are and still be part of the kingdom of God. That's what incarnational theology is all about in my opinion.

For example, one of the important cultural shifts of the past few decades is that multitasking comes naturally to us. We've become polyfocal—able to respond to several things at once. People don't think twice about listening to music while they study or watching a movie while they cook. And yet, our models of worship are still linear and monofocal. Traditional church is like a Broadway musical; periods of dialog and music alternate with each other because it's assumed that the audience can only pay attention to one thing at a time. In film and television, on the other hand, music and text happen simultaneously, both providing narrative and emotional content and both interpreting and enhancing the other.

We need to start thinking about worship music more like a film score. When I write music for a Eucharist, I'll often put music underneath the spoken prayers. I keep the music low and energetic, gradually building through the course of the liturgy, finally climaxing at the passing out of the bread and wine. I want to create a sense of driving anticipation, although I also make sure that the music never covers up the speaking. The music interprets and enhances the liturgy, and it works not only because can people handle multiple things going on at once, but because in our media-drenched culture we almost require it.

*Cheryl Lawrie (phone–Skype):* At its core the church is community of people who are being faithful. The church has been around for over two thousand years and millions of people who have given their lives to changing the world and being faithful to the kingdom. I want to honor that.

*Elise Brown (in person):* Any place where people of faith gather and grow together in their faith, so that they can be agents of transformation in the world. And that does not have to happen in a building. It can happen anywhere with any group of believers who want to come together to grow deeper.

*Kester Brewin (e-mail):* Groups of believers. I'll let others work out the details ;-)

*Ian Mobsby (IM chat) says:* I take inspiration of church as ekklesia—alternative community—the Greek word used in the Roman empire to describe a town council—which was made up of rich men who controlled town politics—well the playful use of this in Christian form—is to live the alternative—as alternative communities that focus on the excluded in society—initially women, children, slaves, and a whole host of

*Ian Mobsby says:* people that were previously excluded—who find a place in the new alternative society—where people are remembered in Christ—that through sacrament—of bread and wine—and remembering Christ—we transform these alternative societies to be empowered by God to transform the world—in modernity we watered all this down to a passive people of God with little power to do anything

*Ian Mobsby says:* this needs to be reframed—drawing on the trinitarian foundation

*Ian Mobsby says:* Anglican churches—need to become wombs of the divine—centered on transformative community centered on love and justice

*Ian Mobsby says:* so we need to reframe church—away from power abuse and cult and back to their true identity as radical places of transformative Christian spirituality worked out

*Ian Mobsby says:* end

# RESOURCES

Recommended Reading—Start the Discussion . . .

Bob Abernathy and William Bole, *The Life of Meaning: Reflections on Faith, Doubt, and Repairing the World* (Seven Stories Press, 2007), http://www.sevenstories.com

Jonny Baker and Doug Gay, *Alternative Worship: Resources from and for the Emerging Church* (book and CD) (Baker Books, 2004), http://www.bakerbooks.com

Diane Butler Bass, *Christianity for the Rest of Us* (HarperSanFrancisco, 2006), http://www.harpercollins.com

Inspired by *The Bible Experience: New Testament* (audio CD) (Zondervan, 2006), http://www.zondervan.com/cultures/en-us/home.htm

Marcus Borg, *The Last Week: What the Gospels Really Teach About Jesus's Final Days in Jerusalem*, repr. ed. (HarperSanFrancisco, 2007), http://www.harpercollins.com

Kester Brewin, *Signs of Emergence: A Vision for Church That Is Always Organic/Networked/Decentralized/Bottom-Up/Communal/Flexible/Always Evolving* (Baker Books, 2007), http://www.emersion books.com

Tom F. Driver, *Liberating Rites: Understanding the Transformative Power of Ritual* (BookSurge, 2006), http://www.booksurge.com

Eddie Gibbs and Ryan K. Bolger, *Emerging Churches: Creating Christian Community in Postmodern Cultures* (Baker Academic, 2005), http://www.bakeracademic.com

Marilyn Haskel, *What Would Jesus Sing?* (Church Publishing, 2007), http://www.churchpublishing.org

Timothy Holder, *Hip Hop Prayer Book* and *The Word Is Hip Hop* (CD) (Church Publishing, 2006), http://www.churchpublishing.org

Daniel Homan, OSB, and Lonni Collins Pratt, *Radical Hospitality: Benedict's Way Of Love* (Paraclete Press, 2005), http://www.paracletepress.com

Roland Howard, *Rise and Fall of the Nine O'clock Service* (Mowbray, 1996), http://www.continuumbooks.com

Tony Jones and Doug Pagitt, eds., *An Emergent Manifesto of Hope* (Baker Books, 2007), http://www.emersionbooks.com

Dan Kimball, David Crowder, and Sally Morgenthaler, *Emerging Worship: Creating Worship Gatherings for New Generations* (Zondervan, 2004), http://www.zondervan.com

Rob Lacy, *the liberator* (Zondervan, 2006), http://www.zondervan.com

——, *The Word on the Street* (book and CD) (Zondervan, 2004), http://www.zondervan.com

C. S. Lewis, *The Screwtape Letters: Anniversary Edition* (audiotapes; read by John Cleese) (Harper SanFrancisco, 1999), http://www.harpercollins.com

Alan Mann, *Atonement for a "Sinless" Society: Engaging with an Emerging Culture* (Paternoster Publishing, 2005), www.paternoster-publishing.com

Alice Mann, *Raising the Roof: The Pastoral-to-Program Size Transition* (Alban Institute, 2001), http://www.alban.org

Brian McLaren, *Everything Must Change: Jesus, Global Crisis, and a Revolution of Hope* (Thomas Nelson, 2007), http://www.thomasnelson.com

——, *Generous Orthodoxy* (Zondervan, 2004), http://www.zondervan.com

——, *The Secret Message of Jesus* (W Publishing, 2006), http://www.thomasnelson.com

Reinhold Niebuhr, *Leaves from the Notebook of a Tamed Cynic* (Westminster John Knox Press, reissue 1991), http://www.ppcbooks.com

Kurt Nielson, *Urban Iona: Celtic Hospitality in the City* (Morehouse Publishing, 2007), http://www.morehousepublishing.org

Jeannine (Jahneen) Otis, *The Gathering* (Church Publishing, 2007), http://www.churchpublishing.org

Martyn Percy and Ian S. Markham, eds., *Why Liberal Churches Are Growing* (Contemporary Christian Culture) (T&T Clark Publishers, 2006), http://www.continuumbooks.com

Christian and Amy Piatt, *MySpace to Sacred Space: God for a New Generation* (Chalice Press, 2007). See www.christianpiatt.com for updated information about Christian's research for this book.

Martha Grace Reese, *Unbinding the Gospel: Real Life Evangelism* (Chalice Press, 2006), http://www.cbp21.com

Peter Rollins, *The Fidelity of Betrayal* (Paraclete Press, 2008), http://www.paracletepress.com

——, *How (Not) to Speak of God* (Paraclete Press, 2006), http://www.paracletepress.com

James K. A. Smith, *Who's Afraid of Postmodernism? Taking Derrida, Lyotard, and Foucault to Church* (Baker Academic, 2006), http://www.bakeracademic.com

Stephanie Spellers, *Radical Welcome: Embracing God, the Other, and the Spirit of Transformation* (Church Publishing, 2006), http://www.churchpublishing.org

Phyllis Tickle, *The Divine Hours*™ (pocket edition) (Oxford University Press, 2007), http://www.oup.com/us

——, *A Great Emergence* (working title) (Baker Books, 2008), http://www.emersionbooks.com

——, *Prayer Is a Place: America's Religious Landscape Observed* (Doubleday, 2005), http://www.randomhouse.com/doubleday

——, *The Words of Jesus: A Gospel of the Sayings of Our Lord with Reflections by Phyllis Tickle* (Jossey-Bass, 2008), http://www.josseybass.com/WileyCDA

Arnold Van Gennep, *The Rites of Passage* (Routledge, 2004), http://www.routledge.com

Miroslav Volf, *Exclusion and Embrace: A Theological Exploration of Identity, Otherness, and Reconciliation* (Abingdon Press, 1996), http://www.abingdonpress.com

Peter Ward, *Liquid Church* (Hendrickson Publishers, 2002), http://www.hendrickson.com

Heath White, *Postmodernism 101: A First Course for the Curious Christian* (Brazos Press, 2006), http://www.brazospress.com

*The Word of Promise: New Testament Audio Bible* (Thomas Nelson, 2007), http://thewordofpromise.com

N. T. Wright, *Evil and the Justice of God* (InterVarsity Press, 2006), http://www.ivpress.com

——, *The Last Word: Beyond the Bible Wars to a New Understanding of the Authority of Scripture* (HarperSanFrancisco, 2005), http://www.harpercollins.com

——, *Simply Christian* (HarperSanFrancisco, 2006), http://www.harpercollins.com

Churches, Organizations, Groups, Places to Visit . . .

## The Alban Institute

An ecumenical, interfaith organization that supports congregations through book publishing, educational seminars, consulting services, and research.

http://www.alban.org

## Allelon

Allelon is a US-based foundation (Boise, Idaho) with a team led by Mark Priddy (Eagle, Idaho) that includes Alan Roxburgh (Vancouver, Canada), Bill Kinnon (Toronto, Canada), Steve Taylor (ChristChurch, New Zealand), Jannie Swart (Johannesburg, South Africa), and others. This multigenerational network of missional church leaders, schools, and parachurch organizations envisions, inspires, engages, resources, trains, and educates leaders for the church and its mission in our culture.

http://www.allelon.org/main.cfm

## Alpha

Fifteen talks addressing key issues relating to the Christian faith followed by small group discussion over a meal. No question is too simple or too hostile.

http://www.alphausa.org

## Alternatives for Simple Living

A nonprofit organization that equips people of faith to challenge consumerism, live justly, and celebrate responsibly.

http://www.simpleliving.org

## Amahoro

Emerging global network named after the African word for peace.

http://amahoro.info

## Anglimergent

To participate in the Anglimergent group, join Facebook (www.facebook.com) and then search under groups for "Anglimergent."

**Calvin Institute of Christian Worship**

Center for study and renewal of worship from a reformed, ecumenical perspective.

http://www.calvin.edu/worship

**Christos Center**

An ecumenical Christian organization, founded in 1978, that offers a preparation program for spiritual direction as well as spiritual directors, workshops, and a spiritual-deepening program. Christos Center is located near St. Paul, Minnesota, and offers distance-learning options.

http://www.christoscenter.org

**Church and Postmodern Culture: Conversation**

Offering discussions of high-profile theorists in postmodern theory and contemporary theology for a nonspecialist audience that is interested in the impact of postmodern theory for the faith and practice of the church.

http://churchandpomo.typepad.com

**Church Marketing Sucks**

Blog designed to frustrate, educate, and motivate the church to communicate, with uncompromising clarity, the truth of Jesus Christ.

http://www.churchmarketingsucks.com

**Church of the Apostles**

A future church with an ancient faith. Their new first CD *Ordo* (music for Eucharist) is available for download and their second CD *Laudamus: Services of Morning and Evening Prayer* is available (CD or electronic files) from www.apostleschurch.org.

**Circle of Hope**

The church for the next generation—a network of cells and communities in Philadelphia, Pennsylvania.

http://www.circleofhope.net

**Common Ground**

Gathering of teachers, artists, business people, seminarians, nannies, musicians, dreamers, cooks, wanderers, and wonderers. They come together in this historic Lutheran church on Manhattan's Upper West

Side to connect with God and one another, to worship in new ways, and to stay down-to-earth.

http://www.myspace.com/advent_commonground

## The Crossing at St. Paul's Boston

The intersection of emerging cultures and ancient Christian traditions of worship, spiritual practice, and community.

http://thecrossingboston.org

## Emergent Village

Growing, generative friendship among missional Christians seeking to love our world in the Spirit of Jesus Christ.

http://www.emergentvillage.com

## Emerging Church Info

A UK-based touching place for the emerging church—sharing stories, reflections, and research.

http://emergingchurch.info

## Emerging Leaders Network

A community of friendship, exploration, and theological conversation among people interested in emerging churches and faith communities.

http://emergingleadersnetwork.org

## Emerging Women Blog

This blog is a space for women involved in the emerging church conversation to use their voice. This is a space to voice your thoughts, express your opinions, and practice your theology. This is a safe community where we can complain, deconstruct, brainstorm, network, dream, and encourage. Let your voice be heard.

http://www.emergingwomen.blogspot.com

## Fresh Expressions

An initiative of the Archbishops of Canterbury and York supported by the Methodist Council. The website features a host of resources, including three booklets: "Moving on in a Mission Shaped Church," "Starting a Fresh Expression," and "Listening for Mission."

http://www.freshexpressions.org.uk

**Fulcrum**

A network of evangelical Anglicans, seeking to renew the center of the evangelical tradition and the center of Anglicanism, acting as a point of balance within the Church of England.

http://www.fulcrum-anglican.org.uk/

**Greenbelt**

A family festival, focusing on arts and faith with music, visual arts, talks, workshops activities, and much more.

http://www.greenbelt.org.uk

**The Haven/NYC**

Christ-centered community of actors, dancers, musicians, writers, directors, artists, educators, dreamers.

http://havennyc.com/index.php

**Hold: This Space**

Tells the story of an alternative worship project in the Uniting Church in Australia, Synod of Victoria, and Tasmania.

http://alternative.victas.uca.org.au

**Ikon**

Inhabiting a space on the outer rim of church experience, Ikon (a group that describes itself as "iconic, apocalyptic, heretical, emerging, and failing") is a Belfast-based collective, who offer anarchic experiments in "transformance art." Challenging the distinction between faith and no faith, Ikon employs a unique and provocative cocktail of music, visual imagery, theatre, ritual and reflection, immersing participants in an experience of theodrama.

http://www.ikon.org.uk

**The Iona Community**

An ecumenical Christian community of men and women from different walks of life and different traditions in the Christian church that is committed to seeking new ways of living the gospel of Jesus Christ in today's world.

http://www.iona.org.uk

### Latino Leadership Circle

A network of ecclesial and marketplace leaders who gather for theological reflection and mutual support. They conduct educational forums, leadership training, and support groups for existing and emerging leaders.

http://latinoleadershipcircle.typepad.com

### Maybe

A young creative community in Oxford, drawing on monastic and contemplative traditions, trying to follow Christ in prayer and action for a better world now.

www.maybe.org.uk

### The MethoBlog

An independent movement of lay and clergy United Methodists engaging in conversation about life, faith, and our common United Methodist Church.

http://methoblog.onlywonder.com/content

### The Moot Community

The online presence for the moot community in Westminster, London, UK. Ian Mobsby's book *Emerging & Fresh Expressions of Church: How Are They Authentically Church & Anglican?* (London: Moot Community Publishing, 2007) can be ordered from http://www.mootique.net. All proceeds benefit The Moot Community.

http://www.moot.uk.net

### Next Wave International

Christian mission to contemporary cultures with a special focus on Europe.

http://www.nextwaveonline.com

### Off the Map

A nonprofit organization that seeks to make evangelism (helping people to connect with God) doable, practical, and fun for ordinary Christians.

http://www.off-the-map.org

## The Ooze

The heart of The Ooze is to encourage the church to engage our emerging culture by developing relationships and resources.

http://www.theooze.com

## Presbymergent

The online community for those who live in both the Presbyterian (PCUSA) and emergent/emerging church worlds.

http://presbymergent.org

## St. Gregory of Nyssa Episcopal Church in San Francisco

Builds creative worship participation from traditional resources, including Eastern Christian resources, with much singing, congregational folk dance, and planned focus on core values. Sophisticated informal style. Historical criticism informs sermon discussion.

http://www.saintgregorys.org

## Saints Peter and Paul Episcopal Church in Portland, Oregon

An Episcopal Christian community in the Catholic tradition, centered on the worship of God in Jesus Christ.

http://www.seekhere.org

## The Simple Way

Our Mission is: "To Love God. To Love people. To Follow Jesus." We're giving that our best shot.

http://thesimpleway.org

## Sites Unseen

A "library of the alternative Christian web," a directory networking more than 5,500 churches, justice movements, contemplative and theology resources, intentional communities, blogs, and webzines dedicated to knowing and following Jesus off the beaten path.

http://zoecarnate.com

## Soliton Network

A global network of cultural creatives, missionaries, activists, church planters, and kingdom entrepreneurs, in dialogue about twenty-first-century mission, justice, spirituality, and the church.

http://www.solitonnetwork.org

**Transmission**

> An underground Manhattan church founded in the summer of 2006; it boasts members who are Catholic, Lutheran, Pentecostal, Episcopal, agnostic, and welcomes all.
>
> http://www.transmissioning.org

**U2 Eucharists**

> An Episcopal Eucharist service that features the music of the rock band U2 and a message about God's call to rally around the UN Millennium Development Goals.
>
> http://u2charist.e4gr.org/index.html

**Urban Seeds**

> An ecumenical initiative based in Melbourne, Australia, seeking renewal of the church and society through engaging faith, community, and culture.
>
> http://seeds.org.au

## A Few Personal Blogs and Websites—Continuing the Dialogue . . .

> Brian McLaren, www.brianmclaren.net
> Cell Phone Spirituality, http://cellphonespirituality.com (Kevin Goodrich's book *Cell Phone Spirituality: What Your Cell Phone Can Teach You about Life and God* [2nd ed., 2007] can be downloaded from this site.)
> Craig Mitchell, http://craigmitchell.typepad.com/mountain_masala
> E~mergent Kiwi, http://www.emergentkiwi.org.nz. Steve Taylor's book *Out of Bounds Church* can be purchased at this site.
> Faith & Theology, http://faith-theology.blogspot.com
> Gareth Higgins, http://godisnotelsewhere.blogspot.com
> The Geranium Farm, http://www.geraniumfarm.org
> Jonny Baker, http://jonnybaker.blogs.com
> Karen Ward, http://submerge.typepad.com
> Kester Brewin, http://kester.typepad.com/signs
> Maggie Dawn, http://maggidawn.typepad.com/maggidawn
> Martha Grace Reese, http://www.GraceNet.info
> Nadia Bolz-Weber, http://www.sarcasticlutheran.typepad.com
> Naked Pastor, http://nakedpastor.com
> Peter Rollins, http://www.ignite.cd/blogs/Pete/index.cfm

Phyllis Tickle, www.phyllistickle.com
Prodigal Kiwi, http://prodigal.typepad.com
Resurrection Life, http://livingtheresurrection.typepad.com
St. Bart's clergy blogs, http://www.stbarts.org/blog.asp
Steve Collins, http://smallritual.blogs.com/small_ritual
TallSkinnyKiwi, http://tallskinnykiwi.typepad.com

## Music, Art, and Other Cool Stuff to Play with . . .

### Church House Publishing

The publishing arm for the Church of England. In particular, check out *Fresh Expressions: The DVD -1: Stories of Church for a Changing Culture* and *Fresh Expressions: The DVD -2: Changing Church in Every Place.*

www.chpublishing.co.uk

### International Day of Peace (September 21) Worship Resources

Join the worldwide movement to create a Global Ceasefire and day of peace and nonviolence.

http://www.internationaldayofpeace.org/resources.htm

### Isaac Everett

Blending electronica, rock, jazz, and middle eastern music with ancient liturgical texts and melodies, Isaac's debut CD *Rotation* is a fresh expression of urban spirituality. *Rotation* can be ordered from CDBaby, Rhapsody, and iTunes. This CD and Isaac's new album will be available on the Proost UK label.

http://www.isaaceverett.com

### Jahneen Otis

Featuring sounds and meditations from this New York–based singer, songwriter, and actress.

http://www.jahneen.com

### Jane Kelly Williams

*Tapping the Wheel* and *The Patchwork of Lost and Found* (CDs) Mercury Records 1995 and Wumi Music Publishing 2000, BMI.

http://www.JaneKellyWilliams.com

### John Francis

Philly based gospel, rock, and folk musician with roots in the Episcopal Church.

http://www.johnfrancismusic.com

### The Ongoing Adventures of ASBO Jesus

Featuring the artwork of Jon Birch. (Note: "asbo" is an "anti-social behavior order" . . . the UK courts award them to people who are deemed to be constant trouble in their neighborhoods . . . presumably according to their neighbors!)

http://asbojesus.wordpress.com

### Potter Street Records

Born in a hallway at The Simple Way Community, Potter Street Records strives to share stories of love, loss, life, hope, and community through the artists on its roster. As indicated by the label's tagline, "Music for the Journey," their goal is to provide a soundtrack for their listeners to inspire and encourage them as they move through life's voyage. Their artists include: Jes Karper, John Mallinen, and Psalters. (See Psalters's CD *The Divine Liturgy of the Wretched Exiles* as per Isaac Everett's recommendation.)

http://www.potterstreetrecords.com

### Proost

Inspiring new resources that fuel faith . . . small collective of creatives using their artistic skills and experience to produce music, images, movies, and words for inspiration, pleasure, and challenge . . . check out Isaac Everett's faves: Ikon, *Dubh* and Proost, Spirit of the New.

http://proost.co.uk

### Taizé

Comprehensive site for those looking for information about the French Taizé community, as well as listing of available resources.

http://www.taize.fr/en

### The Wittenburg Door

The nation's oldest, largest, and only religious satire magazine.

http://wittenburgdoor.com

# ACKNOWLEDGMENTS

This book would not have come about if the late Rev. Judith T. Baumer had not encouraged my involvement with the Live the Faith Weekends at St. Bart's Church back in the 1980s. That was the start of my search for Jesus that led me to meeting the people needed to write this book. Kuddos to Lucas Smith, Church Publishing for helping guide this project to fruition. And a special thanks to everyone in this book for sharing their stories.